OLD TESTAMENT
PROPHETS

A Supplement to the Preacher's Outline & Sermon Bible

King James Version

L EADERSHIP
M INISTRIES W ORLDWIDE

Please address all requests for information or permission to:
Leadership Ministries Worldwide
PO Box 21310
Chattanooga, TN 37424-0310
Ph.# (423) 855-2181   FAX (423) 855-8616   E-Mail info@lmw.org
http://www.lmw.org

Library of Congress Catalog Card Number: 96-75921
International Standard Book Number: 978-1-57407-292-1

Printed in the United States of America

1   2   3   4   5   11   12   13   14   15

DEDICATED

To all the men and women of the world who
preach and teach the Gospel of
our Lord Jesus Christ and
to the Mercy and Grace of God

&

- Demonstrated to us in Christ Jesus our Lord.

  *In him we have redemption through his
  blood, the forgiveness of sins, in accord-
  ance with the riches of God's grace.
  (Ep.1:7)*

- Out of the mercy and grace of God, His Word has
  flowed. Let every person know that God will have
  mercy upon him, forgiving and using him to fulfill
  His glorious plan of salvation.

  *For God so loved the world that he gave
  his one and only Son, that whoever be-
  lieves in him shall not perish but have
  eternal life. For God did not send his Son
  into the world to condemn the world, but to
  save the world through him. (Jn.3:16-17)*

  *This is good, and pleases God our Savior,
  who wants all men to be saved and to come
  to a knowledge of the truth. (1 Ti.2:3-4)*

10/07

The Preacher's Outline & Sermon Bible®

is written for God's servants to use in their study, teaching, and preaching of God's Holy Word…

- to share the Word of God with the world.
- to help believers, both ministers and laypersons, in their understanding, preaching, and teaching of God's Word.
- to do everything we possibly can to lead men, women, boys, and girls to give their hearts and lives to Jesus Christ and to secure the eternal life that He offers.
- to do all we can to minister to the needy of the world.
- to give Jesus Christ His proper place, the place the Word gives Him. Therefore, no work of Leadership Ministries Worldwide—no Outline Bible Resources—will ever be personalized.

THE PROPHETS: THEIR MESSAGE—THEN AND NOW

Dear Friends,

This booklet is a vital resource and companion to *The Preacher's Outline & Sermon Bible* volumes on *Isaiah* through *Malachi*. In it you will find a wealth of information to enhance your preparation of meaningful lessons and/or messages from any of these great books of the Bible.

The prophets were called and chosen by God to do two things:
 ➢ to proclaim God's salvation to man
 ➢ to prophesy and predict how God was going to save man

Both functions were necessary. The prophet had to proclaim salvation to the people of his own generation and to predict how God was going to save the people of all generations. But note: the predictions of the future salvation were not the prophet's own predictions. He had not been called to proclaim his own ideas or message; he had been called to proclaim the salvation of God Himself. He was a man given a very special call, a call to the most important task in all the world: the task of proclaiming the glory and wonder of God's salvation. God was making it possible for man to be saved and to live eternally.

The prophet conveyed the salvation of God...
 • by pointing out the sins of the people
 • by warning the people about the terrible and certain consequences of sin, the discipline and judgment of God
 • by encouraging the people to repent by wholeheartedly turning back to God, worshipping Him and Him alone
 • by proclaiming God's eternal plan of salvation and blessings to those who would believe

Speaking of the prophets, Peter Adams writes, "To respond to God's words is to respond to God."[1]

"But those things, which God before had showed by the mouth of all his prophets, that Christ should suffer, he hath so fulfilled. Repent ye therefore, and be converted, that your sins may be blotted out, when the times of refreshing shall come from the presence of the Lord; And he shall send Jesus Christ, which before was preached unto you: Whom the heaven must receive until the times of restitution of all things, which God hath spoken by the mouth of all his holy prophets since the world began. For Moses truly said unto the fathers, A prophet shall the Lord your God raise up unto you of your brethren, like unto me; him shall ye hear in all things whatsoever he shall say unto you. And it shall come to pass, that every soul, which will not hear that prophet, shall be destroyed from among the people. Yea, and all the prophets from Samuel and those that follow after, as many as have spoken, have likewise foretold of these days. Ye are the children of the prophets, and of the covenant which God made with our fathers, saying unto Abraham, And in thy seed shall all the kindreds of the earth be blessed. Unto you first God, having raised up his Son Jesus, sent him to bless you, in turning away every one of you from his iniquities" (Ac.3:18-26).

The Books of the Bible written by the prophets of God contain as many valuable lessons for today's believers as they had for those to whom the prophets originally spoke. It is our prayer that this booklet will enrich your study and your message in a way that will bless all who hear as it helps them grow in faithfulness.

Your fellow servants at...

LEADERSHIP MINISTRIES WORLDWIDE

---

[1] Peter Adams. *Speaking God's Words.* (Downers Grove, IL: Inter-Varsity Press, 1996), pp.19-20.

ALPHABETICAL LISTING OF THE PROPHETS

NAME	DATE
Abel	Right after creation
Abraham	2000 B.C.
Agabus	A.D. 43
Ahijah	931–910 B.C.
Amos	750 B.C.
Anna	4 B.C.
Asaph	1004 B.C.
Azariah	896 B.C.
Daniel	605–535 B.C.
David	1029–971 B.C.
Deborah	1220 B.C.
Eliezer	849–848 B.C.
Elijah	860–845 B.C.
Elisha	850–795 B.C.
Ezekiel	593–571 B.C.
Gad	1015–950 B.C.
Habakkuk	615–598 B.C.
Haggai	520 B.C.
Hanani	870 B.C.
Heman	971 B.C.
Hosea	788–723 B.C.
Huldah	623 B.C.
Iddo	910 B.C.
Isaiah	740–690 B.C.
Jacob/Israel	1858 B.C.
Jehu	886 B.C.
Jeremiah	627–562 B.C.
Joel	830 B.C.
John the Apostle	A.D. 95
John the Baptist	A.D. 26
Jonah	780–765 B.C.
Joseph	1900–1885 B.C.
Malachi	430 B.C.
Micah	735–725 B.C.
Micaiah	853 B.C.
Moses	1405 B.C.

NAME	DATE
Nahum	663–612 B.C.
Nathan	1003–931 B.C.
Noah	At least seven generations after Adam
Obadiah	845 B.C.
Oded	733 B.C.
Paul	A.D. 35–64
Shemaiah	926 B.C.
Unnamed prophet Prophesied a total victory over the Syrians	855 B.C.
Unnamed prophet Prophesied a victory over the Syrians	856 B.C.
Unnamed prophet Rebuked Eli and his house for profaning the temple	1085 B.C.
Unnamed prophet Rebuked Israel for fearing idols	1210 B.C.
Unnamed prophet Rebuked King Ahab for sparing the evil Ben-Hadad	855 B.C.
Unnamed prophet Rebuked King Amaziah for his idolatry	767 B.C.
Unnamed prophet Rebuked King Jeroboam I for his idolatry	931 B.C.
Unnamed prophet Warned King Amaziah not to hire Israel's army	767 B.C.
Urijah	608 B.C.
Zechariah, son of Jehoiada	797 B.C.
Zephaniah	640–609 B.C.

THE PROPHETS

CHRONOLOGICAL LISTING OF THE PROPHETS[2]

NAME	DATE
Abel	Right after creation
Noah	At least seven generations after Adam
Abraham	2000 B.C.
Joseph	1900–1885 B.C.
Jacob/Israel	1858 B.C.
Moses	1405 B.C.
Deborah	1220 B.C.
Unnamed prophet Rebuked Israel for fearing idols	1210 B.C.
Samuel	1095–1015 B.C.
Unnamed prophet Rebuked Eli and his house for profaning the temple	1085 B.C.
David	1029–971 B.C.
Gad	1015–950 B.C.
Asaph	1004 B.C.
Nathan	1003–931 B.C.
Heman	971 B.C.
Unnamed prophet Rebuked King Jeroboam I for his idolatry	931 B.C.
Ahijah	931–910 B.C.
Shemaiah	926 B.C.
Iddo	910 B.C.
Azariah	896 B.C.
Jehu	886 B.C.
Hanani	870 B.C.
Elijah	860–845 B.C.
Unnamed prophet Prophesied a victory over the Syrians	856 B.C.
Unnamed prophet Prophesied total victory over the Syrians	855 B.C.
Unnamed prophet Rebuked King Ahab for sparing the evil Ben-Hadad	855 B.C.

NAME	DATE
Micaiah	853 B.C.
Elisha	850–795 B.C.
Eliezer	849–848 B.C.
Obadiah	845 B.C.
Joel	830 B.C.
Zechariah, son of Jehoiada	797 B.C.
Hosea	788–723 B.C.
Jonah	780–765 B.C.
Unnamed prophet Rebuked King Amaziah for his idolatry	767 B.C.
Unnamed prophet Warned King Amaziah not to hire Israel's army	767 B.C.
Amos	750 B.C.
Isaiah	740–690 B.C.
Micah	735–725 B.C.
Oded	733 B.C.
Nahum	663–612 B.C.
Zephaniah	640–609 B.C.
Jeremiah	627–562 B.C.
Huldah	623 B.C.
Habakkuk	615–598 B.C.
Urijah	608 B.C.
Daniel	605–535 B.C.
Ezekiel	593–571 B.C.
Haggai	520 B.C.
Zechariah, son of Berechiah	520–518 B.C.
Malachi	430 B.C.
Anna	4 B.C.
John the Baptist	A.D. 26
Paul	A.D. 35–64
Agabus	A.D. 43
John the Apostle	A.D. 95

---

[2] The list above serves as a timeline for all the prophets discussed in the following chart. The unnamed prophets are listed according to their message. (Also see the *Timeline of Kings, Prophets, and History* chart, pp.392-393.)

PROPHET	TIME/PLACE GIVEN	MAIN MESSAGE	PRACTICAL APPLICATION
ABEL (Breath) **Known Facts** 1. Was the son of Adam (Ge.4:2). 2. Was called a prophet by Jesus Christ (Mt. 23:34-35; Lu. 11:50-51). 3. Kept the flocks of animals (Ge.4:2). 4. Brought an acceptable and pleasing sacrifice to God (Ge. 4:4). 5. Was murdered by his brother, Cain (Ge.4:8). 6. Was avenged by God (Ge.4:9-12). **Predictions and Messages** By example he taught that a person must approach God through the sacrifice of a substitute offering (Ge.4:4). **Scripture References** Ge.4:1-16; Mt.23:34-39; Lu.11:47-51; He.11:4; 12:24	**Time** *The first years after creation, when Adam was still alive.* **Place** *Outside the garden of Eden, where man first began to farm.*	Abel's message is seen in his worship. Note what Abel did: when he approached the LORD, he brought an animal, a blood sacrifice. Why? Because his father, Adam, had taught him to approach God through the sacrifice of an animal. God taught Adam... • that sin causes death • that an innocent substitute had to sacrificially die in order to clothe man's shame and guilt • that thereafter man could only approach God through the sacrificial death of an innocent substitute Thus Abel pointed forward to Christ, the perfect sacrifice. He may not have completely understood, but Abel did approach God through the blood sacrifice, just as his father had taught him. Abel had *faith*. He believed that God would forgive his sins and accept him through the sacrifice of an innocent life. And note the remarkable testimony Scripture gives about Abel's faith in the coming Savior: Abel even today, although dead, testifies of Christ (He.11:4). What a striking legacy Abel left to the world! **"And Abel, he also brought of the firstlings of his flock and of the fat thereof. And the LORD had respect unto Abel and to his offering" (Ge.4:4).** **"By faith Abel offered unto God a more excellent sacrifice than Cain, by which he obtained witness that he was righteous, God testifying of his gifts: and by it he being dead yet speaketh" (He.11:4).** **"And to Jesus the mediator of the new covenant, and to the blood of sprinkling, that speaketh better things than that of Abel" (He.12:24).**	No person can earn, win, or merit salvation. No person can approach God through his own works, energy, efforts, fruits, ways, religion, ceremony or ritual. The reason is clearly evident: no person is perfect. We have a sin problem and a death problem that has to be taken care of before we can ever become acceptable to God. God has taken care of this in the sacrifice of His Son for our sins. Jesus Christ took our sins upon Himself and died for them. This is what the sacrifice of the innocent life symbolized in the Old Testament. Just like Abel, we must believe God, believe that the death (the blood) of the sacrifice of Jesus Christ covers our sins. God accepts no person apart from Jesus Christ, the promised seed and Savior of the world. God has never accepted *any person* apart from the shedding of the blood of His dear Son. The blood of Christ had to be shed for all persons through all the generations of human history. Apart from Christ, apart from accepting His sacrifice, no person can be saved from sin. No person can escape the judgment of death and hell apart from Christ. **"Ye serpents, ye generation of vipers, how can ye escape the damnation of hell?" (Mt.23:33).** **"For when we were yet without strength, in due time Christ died for the ungodly" (Ro.5:6).** **"For I delivered unto you first of all that which I also received, how that Christ died for our sins according to the scriptures" (1 Co.15:3).** **"And walk in love, as Christ also hath loved us, and hath given himself for us an offering and a sacrifice to God for a sweetsmelling savour" (Ep.5:2).**

PROPHET	TIME/PLACE GIVEN	MAIN MESSAGE	PRACTICAL APPLICATION
AGABUS (Locust) **Known Facts** 1. Lived in Judea near Jerusalem (Ac.21:10). 2. Ministered among a company of prophets (Ac.11:27-28). 3. Prophesied with the words of the Holy Spirit (Ac.11:28; 21:11). 4. Spoke for the prophets (Ac.11:28). **Predictions and Messages** 1. A severe famine would come to the entire Roman world (Ac.11:28). 2. The Apostle Paul would be bound and taken prisoner, and eventually killed (Ac. 21:11-13). **Scripture References** Ac.11:27-30; 21:10-14	**Time** *A.D. 43, at the beginning of the terrible persecution of Agrippa.* **Place** *Antioch of Syria, where the followers of Jesus Christ were first called Christians.*	Agabus prophesied two future events by the Spirit of God. First, Agabus prophesied that a great famine would occur. The disciples accepted the message given and gathered funds and stores of food to be used for those in need. Note this fact: the disciples did not waste time questioning God; they simply acted immediately on the information given, doing what was necessary for the church to continue. Some time later, Agabus prophesied that the Gentiles (or Romans) would take the Apostle Paul prisoner. Despite the danger of suffering and persecution, and eventually death, Paul was unhindered in his mission to preach the gospel. Knowing the prophecy, the fire of devotion within Paul burned all the more. Why? Because Paul trusted God. He understood that nothing is out of God's control. He firmly believed that as long as he continued to do the will of the Lord, the Lord would richly bless his labor for the gospel. **"And in these days came prophets from Jerusalem unto Antioch. And there stood up one of them named Agabus, and signified by the Spirit that there should be great dearth throughout all the world" (Ac.11:27-28).** **"And as we tarried there many days, there came down from Judaea a certain prophet, named Agabus. And when he was come unto us, he took Paul's girdle, and bound his own hands and feet, and said, Thus saith the Holy Ghost, So shall the Jews at Jerusalem bind the man that owneth this girdle, and shall deliver him into the hands of the Gentiles" (Ac.21:10-11).**	1. Giving is essential. Believers must give to those in need. And they should practice regular giving, not waiting for some disaster to strike and then scrambling for a solution to the problem. Giving should be a regular habit of the believer so the mission of the church can be carried out, even in difficult times. 2. Believers will suffer. Believers suffer by: ➤ being ridiculed ➤ being mocked ➤ being assaulted ➤ being spoken evil of ➤ being gossiped about ➤ being slandered ➤ being reviled ➤ being insulted ➤ being scolded ➤ being falsely accused ➤ being put on trial ➤ even being murdered But suffering is necessary. First of all, believers must live out the calling given to them by the Lord no matter how unpleasant, no matter what the cost. Second, suffering prepares the believer to participate in the glory of Christ. It is the necessary condition for exaltation. Suffering and struggling are a refining process through which the believer must pass. It refines the believer by forcing him to expand his trust in God more and more. Suffering drives a believer to cast himself more and more upon the care of God; therefore, the believer moves closer and closer to the Lord praying, worshipping and fellowshipping with him more and more. God is in complete control of every situation. Sometimes He allows unpleasant trials to come our way, but this is all according to His will, according to His plan for our lives. We must trust God no matter what and do all we can to understand His will and to do it. **"Yea, and all that will live godly in Christ Jesus shall suffer persecution" (2 Ti.3:12).** **"For unto you it is given in the behalf of Christ, not only to believe on him, but also to suffer for his sake" (Ph.1:29).** **"Wherein ye greatly rejoice, though now for a season, if need be, ye are in heaviness through manifold temptations: That the trial of your faith, being much more precious than of gold that perisheth, though it be tried with fire, might be found unto praise and honour and glory at the appearing of Jesus Christ" (1 Pe.1:6-7).**

PROPHET	TIME/PLACE GIVEN	MAIN MESSAGE	PRACTICAL APPLICATION
AHIJAH (Brother in Jehovah/Yahweh) **THE SHILONITE** **Known Facts** 1. Lived in Shiloh (1 K. 11:29). 2. Called to minister during the time of Solomon and Jeroboam (1 K.11:28-29). 3. Became blind in his old age (1 K.14:4). **Predictions and Messages** 1. The division of the nation of Israel into two kingdoms—the Northern Kingdom of Israel and the Southern Kingdom of Judah (1 K.11:31). 2. The death of Abijah, the son of King Jeroboam (1 K.14:9-13). 3. The destruction of the entire family of King Jeroboam (1 K. 14:10-13). 4. The captivity and exile of Israel to a foreign land (1 K. 14:14-16). **Scripture References** 1 K.11:29-39; 12:15; 14:4-16; 2 Chr.9:29	**Time** *The end of Solomon's reign, just before 931 B.C. until 910 B.C., near the end of the reign of Jeroboam I.* **Place** *Ahijah's first prophecy was given in the countryside, just outside Jerusalem.* *Later, after the division of the kingdom, Ahijah ministered in his hometown of Shiloh, preaching mainly to the Northern Kingdom of Israel.*	Israel was divided because the king and people had forsaken God, engaged in false worship, disobeyed God's commandments and refused to walk in the ways of the LORD. Jeroboam, Solomon's very own trusted servant, became king over the Northern Kingdom just as Ahijah predicted. But when King Jeroboam displayed a life of wickedness and idolatry, judgment fell on him and on his entire household, beginning with the immediate death of his own son. Eventually, all Israel would go into captivity, because they would not repent of their wickedness, nor turn from the state religion of idolatry and false worship instituted by Jerusalem. **"And he said to Jeroboam, Take thee ten pieces: for thus saith the LORD, the God of Israel, Behold, I will rend the kingdom out of the hand of Solomon, and will give ten tribes to thee" (1 K.11:31).** **"But [you] hast done evil above all that were before thee: for thou hast gone and made thee other gods, and molten images, to provoke me to anger, and hast cast me behind thy back: Therefore, behold, I will bring evil upon the house of Jeroboam,"...Arise thou therefore, get thee to thine own house:** *and* **when thy feet enter into the city, the child shall die. ...For the LORD shall smite Israel, as a reed is shaken in the water, and he shall root up Israel out of this good land, which he gave to their fathers, and shall scatter them beyond the river, because they have made their groves, provoking the LORD to anger" (1 K. 14:9-10, 12, 15).**	If we continue in sin and wickedness and become involved in false worship, we will face the judgment of God. God will chastise and discipline us in order to bring us back to Him. God is zealous for us and will not allow us to chase after worldly affections, not for long. If we refuse to repent, we will face the judgment of God's hand. Even future generations may suffer and bear the brunt of our sins, suffering the great and terrible consequences of God's wrath. **"The LORD knoweth how to deliver the godly out of temptations, and to reserve the unjust unto the day of judgment to be punished" (2 Pe.2:9).** **"Every branch in me that beareth not fruit he taketh away: and every branch that beareth fruit, he purgeth it, that it may bring forth more fruit" (Jn.15:2).** **"My son, despise not the chastening of the LORD; neither be weary of his correction: For whom the LORD loveth he correcteth; even as a father the son in whom he delighteth" (Pr. 3:11-12).** **"Thou shalt not bow down thyself to them, nor serve them: for I the LORD thy God am a jealous God, visiting the iniquity of the fathers upon the children unto the third and fourth generation of them that hate me; And showing mercy unto thousands of them that love me, and keep my commandments" (Ex.20:5-6).**

PROPHET	TIME/PLACE GIVEN	MAIN MESSAGE	PRACTICAL APPLICATION
AMOS (Burden-bearer) **Known Facts** 1. Lived in Tekoa, on the edge of the Judean desert (Am.1:1). 2. Worked as a shepherd and as a farmer of sycamore trees (Am.1:1; 7:14). 3. Wrote the book of *Amos*. 4. Preached fiery sermons and saw startling visions. **Predictions and Messages** 1. A sermon about God's coming judgment on sinful nations, including Israel (Am.1:1-4:13). 2. A sermon about the need for seeking God with the whole heart (Am.5:1-27). 3. A sermon warning the people not to be greedy (Am.6:4-14). 4. The vision of locusts—a picture of the crops being destroyed by the ferocious insects, but Amos interceded and God had mercy (Am.7:1-3). 5. The vision of fire—a picture of the fields being destroyed, but Amos interceded and God had mercy (Am.7:4-5). 6. The vision of a plumb line—a picture of the crookedness of Israel (Am.7:7-9). 7. The vision of a basket of fruit—a picture of the rottenness of Israel's sin (Am.8:1-3). 8. A sermon warning that God will severely judge those who treat the poor unfairly (Am.8:4-14). 9. The vision of the LORD standing on the altar, striking His own temple (Am.9:1-10). 10. The prophecy about the captivity and return of Israel (Am.9:9-15). **Scripture References** The book of *Amos*	**Time** *About 750 B.C., near the end of the rule of Jeroboam II in Israel and during the long reign of Uzziah in Judah.* *The time in which Amos preached was a very prosperous time economically and financially for the people of Israel, but not spiritually. Spiritually the hearts of the people were filled with greed, so much so that they oppressed the poor without mercy.* **Place** *Israel, the Northern Kingdom.*	God will judge sin wherever it is found. No sinner is exempt from judgment. Without genuine repentance, God's judgment will surely fall upon the sinner. Amos focused upon one theme, one subject: the coming judgment of God upon those who refused to turn from sin. Despite persecution and death threats, Amos faithfully continued to preach the messages given him by God, a series of blistering sermons against the sins of arrogance and pride. **"Therefore thus will I do unto thee, O Israel: and because I will do this unto thee, prepare to meet thy God, O Israel" (Am. 4:12).** **"Then answered Amos, and said to Amaziah, I was no prophet, neither was I a prophet's son; but I was an herdman, and a gatherer of sycamore fruit: And the LORD took me as I followed the flock, and the LORD said unto me, Go, prophesy unto my people Israel" (Am.7:14-15).**	Worldly gain, such as riches, social position, heritage, even religion will not save a person. Such things can be good if they are used to help the poor or advance God's kingdom. But when a person uses worldly gain just for the purpose of more worldly gain, God's judgment is sure to fall upon that person. At least two major applications can be seen in the prophecies of Amos. 1. Just think of the people gripped by greed who push aside the needs of others... • to make themselves more comfortable • to buy some luxury • to enjoy more leisure time • to hoard more riches Shockingly, some people are so gripped by greed, they even assault and murder in order to gain more and more. Unbelievably, they consider human life worthless if it stands in the way of their gaining more riches. 2. The minister of God must boldly preach the Word of God. He must not form his sermon based on what people want to hear, nor avoid certain subjects because he will not be popular. The messenger of the LORD must be unashamed and unswerving in his calling to preach the whole counsel of God. Even persecution, no matter how serious, must not prevent the minister from proclaiming the Word of God, declaring what God has anointed him to say. **"Charge them that are rich in this world, that they be not highminded, nor trust in uncertain riches, but in the living God, who giveth us richly all things to enjoy" (1 Ti.6:17).** **"I charge thee therefore before God, and the Lord Jesus Christ, who shall judge the quick [living] and the dead at his appearing and his kingdom; preach the word; be instant in season, out of season; reprove, rebuke, exhort with all longsuffering and doctrine" (2 Ti.1:3-4).**

PROPHET	TIME/PLACE GIVEN	MAIN MESSAGE	PRACTICAL APPLICATION
ANNA **(Gracious)** **Known Facts** 1. Served in the temple as a woman prophet (Lu.2:36). 2. Appeared as the first prophet since Malachi, a space of over 300 years. 3. Descended from the tribe of Asher (Lu. 2:36). 4. Widowed for many years (Lu.2:36). 5. Fasted and prayed continually (Lu.2:37). 6. Loved and hoped in God, therefore she was blessed (Lu.2:37). 7. Pointed out Christ to others (Lu.2:38). **Predictions and Messages** Jesus is the Christ, the Savior of the world (Lu.2:38). **Scripture References** Lu.2:36-38	**Time** *About 4 B.C., eight days after the birth of Jesus Christ.* **Place** *At the temple in Jerusalem.*	Anna's message was the greatest of all messages: Jesus Christ is the Redeemer, the promised Messiah Who brings redemption to all who ask for God's salvation. Anna shared this good news with anyone looking for redemption in Jerusalem. **"And she coming in that instant gave thanks likewise unto the Lord, and spake of him [the Christ child] to all them that looked for redemption in Jerusalem" (Lu.2:38).**	1. God will greatly bless the person who places his entire hope in Him. God will always bless the person who trusts in Him. We must rely on God for our salvation, rely on Him with our whole heart, holding nothing back, seeking Him continually. For there is no other person, no other place, no other source to whom we can turn for the salvation of our soul. Salvation is in Christ, and Christ alone. 2. Believers should be busy talking to everyone about Jesus Christ, for Jesus Christ came to earth to redeem us from our sins. And He will grant forgiveness to anyone who seeks for it, to anyone who will place his entire hope in the Lord. **"Behold the eye of the Lord is upon them that fear him, upon them that hope in his mercy" (Ps.33:18).** **"Being justified freely by his grace through the redemption that is in Christ Jesus" (Ro.3:24).**
ASAPH **(Gathering)** **Known Facts** 1. Was the son of Berechiah (1 Chr.6:39). 2. Descended from the tribe of Levi and the clan of Kohathites (1 Chr.6:33, 39). 3. Appointed by David as a musician, Asaph played the cymbals and sang (1 Chr. 6:31, 39). 4. Called a Seer (2 Chr. 29:30). 5. Wrote lyrics which were used many years after his death (2 Chr. 29:30). **Predictions and Messages** Sang and played music to praise and glorify the LORD. **Scripture References** 1 Chr.6:31-43; 15:17-19 2 Chr.29:30	**Time** *1004 B.C. Right after David was first crowned king in Hebron, he decided to bring the Ark of the Covenant from Kiriath-Jearim to Jerusalem. It was at this time that Asaph and the other musicians were appointed by King David to lead the people of Israel in worship, praising the LORD in songs of praise and celebration to the LORD.* **Place** *Jerusalem, the Holy City.*	Asaph was one of the leading musicians during the days of King David. Although there is not any specific message recorded by Asaph, he lived a life of praise and worship and greatly encouraged others to do so. Down through the years, Asaph's testimony was that of leading and encouraging the congregation in praising the LORD. **"So the Levites appointed Heman the son of Joel; and of his brethren, Asaph the son of Berechiah; and of the sons of Merari their brethren, Ethan the son of Kushaiah" (1 Chr.15:17).** **"Moreover Hezekiah the king and the princes commanded the Levites to sing praise unto the LORD with the words of David, and of Asaph the seer. And they sang praises with gladness, and they bowed their heads and worshipped" (2 Chr.29:30).**	The importance of praise and worship cannot be overstressed. As the Creator of the universe, the LORD expects us to praise and worship Him. It is the LORD Who has created life and Who sustains life. The air we breathe, the water we drink, the food we eat—every good and perfect gift we have comes from the hand of the LORD with Whom there is no changing. Because of all the richness and depth of all the blessings God pours out upon us—because of all the good and perfect gifts He so mercifully gives every day of our lives—the LORD expects, and rightly deserves, our worship and the praise of His holy name. **"Oh that men would praise the LORD for his goodness, and for his wonderful works to the children of men!" (Ps.107:8, 15, 21, 31).** **"Blessed be the Lord, who daily loadeth us with benefits, even the God of our salvation. Selah" (Ps.68:19).**

PROPHET	TIME/PLACE GIVEN	MAIN MESSAGE	PRACTICAL APPLICATION
AZARIAH (Jehovah/Yahweh is my Helper) **Known Facts** 1. Was the son of Oded (2 Chr.15:1). 2. Ministered as the first of the prophets to the Southern Kingdom of Judah after the division of the nation of Israel. **Predictions and Messages** Azariah instructed King Asa to extend the revival which had begun in the land. Asa was not to lose courage, but to continue to serve God with fervor (2 Chr.15:2-7). **Scripture References** 2 Chr.15:1-12	**Time** *896 B.C., during the reign of Asa, king of Judah, who stirred a great reformation and revival among the people.* **Place** *Jerusalem, the Holy City and capital of Judah.*	Revival was sweeping through the land of Judah resulting in changed lives and a reformation of worship. King Asa and his troops had just delivered a crushing defeat to the invading Ethiopians. But right afterward, Asa was tempted to rely on his own strength. So Azariah, the prophet, pressed the king and the people to seek the LORD more than ever before. He challenged them not to fall into a foolish and destructive attitude of pride and self-reliance. Azariah declared that the LORD wanted the people to be as strong spiritually as they had been in battle. King Asa responded to Azariah's message and continued to stir a strong reformation among the people. He removed the pagan images of idolatry as well as those in charge of their worship. Then, he made all false worship illegal, instituting the death penalty for all who practiced it. Committing himself totally to the LORD, he established the purity of true worship, the worship of the LORD God alone (Jehovah/Yahweh). **"Now the Spirit of God came on Azariah the son of Oded, and he went out to meet Asa and said to him, "Listen to me, Asa, and all Judah and Benjamin: the LORD is with you when you are with Him. And if you seek Him, He will let you find Him; but if you forsake Him, He will forsake you... be strong and do not lose courage, for there is reward for your work" (2 Chr.15:1-2, 7).**	Seeking the LORD is essential for every believer. We must seek Him with our whole heart, seek Him continually. Anything that could trap us in a deadly snare of sin must be removed. Placing God first in our lives, first in everything we do, must be our never-ending effort. We must draw close to the LORD, as close as we possibly can. We must continue to stoke the fire of revival in our hearts, to let it burn hotter and hotter. Why? Because we are always in need, in very desperate need, of God's help. Even when things seem to be going smoothly, we need God. We need Him... • for daily guidance • for spiritual strength • to escape temptation • for our daily food • to hold the world together • for our very next breath • for *all* our needs, *for every single need, every day of our lives* And remember this: God will *actively move in the behalf of the one who seeks Him*. Our labor is not in vain. There is a reward for serving God. God strongly supports those who wholeheartedly serve Him. **"And let us not be weary in well doing: for in due season we shall reap, if we faint not" (Ga.6:9).** **"But seek ye first the kingdom of God, and his righteousness; and all these things shall be added unto you" (Mt.6:33).** **"For the eyes of the Lord run to and fro throughout the whole earth to show himself strong in the behalf of them whose heart is perfect toward him" (2 Chr.16:9).**

PROPHET	TIME/PLACE GIVEN	MAIN MESSAGE	PRACTICAL APPLICATION
DANIEL **(God is my Judge)** **Known Facts** 1. Was taken captive by the Babylonians and forced to live in Babylon (Da.1:1-2). 2. Prophesied to three major world powers—Israel, Babylon and Medo-Persia (Da.1:1-2; 5:31). 3. Possessed tremendous integrity (Da.1:8-10; 6:4; Eze.14:1). 4. Was given a Babylonian name (Belteshazzar) because he was highly favored among the exiles, and because he needed to conduct business in Babylon (Da.1:7). 5. Was able to understand all kinds of mysteries (Da.7:15-28; 8:15-27; 9:24-27; 10:1-14; Eze.28:3). 6. Was delivered miraculously from the den of lions (Da.6:19-23). 7. Saw strange and vivid visions about Israel's future, about the coming dominant world powers of human history, and about a future period of history known as the *Great Tribulation* and the end of the world (Da.7:1–12:13). 8. Wrote the book of *Daniel*. **Predictions and Messages** 1. The interpretation of King Nebuchadnezzar's dream of a great statue, which symbolizes the coming great world powers (Da.2:17-19). 2. The interpretation of King Nebuchadnezzar's dream of a great tree which predicted the coming judgment against Nebuchadnezzar due to his pride (Da.4:19-27). (Cont. on next page)	**Time** *605–535 B.C., during the Babylonian captivity of Judah and on into the first years of the Medo-Persian Empire. Daniel was just a young man, only about thirty years old when he was taken captive. He lived the rest of his days in Babylon, ministering to his people, serving as a statesman for Babylon and recording history, writing down his visions and prophecies of the future.* **Place** *Near the Tigris River during the last years of the Babylonian Empire and the first few years of the Medo-Persian Empire.*	The book of *Daniel* has one unmistakable message: God sets up kings and puts down kings. The powers of the world will struggle and struggle to gain domination, wealth, and control; but God is in control and overrules everything they do, working all things out for the good of genuine believers and accomplishing His will for the world. Only He can exalt or humble; only He can deliver or destroy. God is sovereign over all. He lifts up those who acknowledge His sovereignty and puts down those who become filled with pride and self-sufficiency. After the end of the Assyrian Empire, control passed mainly to Babylon, which had been firmly established by Nabopolassar. Nabopolassar's son (Nebuchadnezzar II, the king we read about in the book of *Daniel*) then took over. The first thing Nebuchadnezzar did was to export most of the Judeans to Babylon. This included Daniel and his three friends. But despite their new pagan surroundings, Daniel and his three friends became very successful and were highly esteemed by the Babylonians. This was due to God's guidance, for they remained faithful to the LORD and to Him alone. Daniel became a close advisor and statesman for Nebuchadnezzar. Through the interpretation of dreams, which God inflicted upon the king, Daniel was lifted to a very high position in the Babylonian kingdom. Years later, Nebuchadnezzar's grandson Belshazzar became king. He was prideful like his grandfather before him. But there was a difference. Nebuchadnezzar repented and acknowledged God as the Sovereign over the earth, but Belshazzar refused to do so. The last straw came when Belshazzar defiled the articles of the temple of God by using them at a drunken feast in honor of a false god. At this, God literally wrote on the wall with His finger, burning a permanent message of immediate doom upon the king and the Babylonian empire. Belshazzar was slain that night as the Medo-Persian soldiers stormed the capital and the palace, and the new empire was put in place.	➢ All the world is to praise God for His holiness. ➢ All the world is to praise God for His sovereignty and omnipotence. ➢ All the world is to praise God for His eternal existence. What an indictment against man! How little we praise and worship God—truly praise and worship Him. Think for a moment and imagine in your mind the four beings who surround the throne of God. They were created to worship God, and they worship Him day and night, never ceasing from worshipping Him. They cry out day and night the glorious praise: "Holy, holy, holy, Lord God Almighty, which was, and is, and is to come" (Re. 4:8). The very thought of such a scene should bring us to our knees in repentance, humility and worship of God and His Son, Jesus Christ, the King of kings and Lord of lords. What a lesson the book of *Daniel* has for us! For the LORD God Almighty dwells in glory and majesty, dominion, and power. We owe Him our lives, all we are and have. **"Exalt the LORD our God, and worship at his holy hill; for the LORD our God is holy" (Ps.99:9).** **"And one cried unto another, and said, Holy, holy, holy, is the LORD of hosts: the whole earth is full of his glory" (Is.6:3).** **"Who shall not fear thee, O Lord, and glorify thy name? for thou only art holy: for all nations shall come and worship before thee; for thy judgments are made manifest" (Re.15:4).** **"For I am the LORD that bringeth you up out of the land of Egypt, to be your God: ye shall therefore be holy, for I am holy" (Lev.11:45).** **"I know that thou canst do every thing, and that no thought can be withholden from thee" (Jb.42:2).** **"But our God is in the heavens: he hath done whatsoever he hath pleased" (Ps.115:3).** **"Yea, before the day was I am he; and there is none that can deliver out of my hand: I will work, and who shall let [hinder] it?" (Is.43:13).**

PROPHET	TIME/PLACE GIVEN	MAIN MESSAGE	PRACTICAL APPLICATION
DANIEL (cont.) 3. The message that God gives political power to whomever He wishes (Da.4:25). 4. The interpretation of the handwriting on the wall written to King Belshazzar by the finger of God Himself—the prediction of the soon coming judgment against Belshazzar and the end of the Babylonian Empire (Da.5:10-28). 5. The vision of the four beasts arising from the sea—a prophecy of the coming dominant world powers (Da.7:1-8). 6. The vision of Jesus Christ, the Ancient of Days (Da.7:9-10; Re. 4:4; Mt.19:28; 1 Co.6:3). 7. The vision of the fourth beast being destroyed—the prophecy about the defeat of the antichrist (Da.7:11-12). 8. The vision of Jesus Christ—One like the Son of Man (Da. 7:13-14). 9. The vision of the ram and the two horns—a prophecy of the end of the Medo-Persian Empire and the rise of the Greek Empire (Da.8:1-14). 10. The message from Gabriel about Jeremiah's seventy weeks—the prediction that the Messiah, Jesus Christ, the Savior of the world, would be rejected 483 years in the future (Da.9:24-26). 11. The message from Gabriel about Jeremiah's seventieth week—the prediction of the coming Tribulation, the desecration of the temple by the antichrist and the end of the world (Da.9:26-27; Mt.24:15-25; Mk. 13:14-23). (Cont. on next page)		But Daniel, who continued to give God honor and to remain humble, was quickly lifted up to a high rank in the government of the Medes. Both before and after the change in power, Daniel saw amazing visions and received many startling messages from angels about the powers of the world, both present and future, and about the end times. Daniel wrote down many of these, but was instructed to withhold others. In all of his writings, Daniel continually proclaimed the great majesty of God and the need to honor Him. **"This is the dream; and we will tell the interpretation thereof before the king. Thou, O king, art a king of kings: for the God of heaven hath given thee a kingdom, power, and strength, and glory. And wheresoever the children of men dwell, the beasts of the field and the fowls of the heaven hath he given into thine hand, and hath made thee ruler over them all. Thou art this head of gold. And after thee shall arise another kingdom inferior to thee, and another third kingdom of brass, which shall bear rule over all the earth. And the fourth kingdom shall be strong as iron: forasmuch as iron breaketh in pieces and subdueth all things: and as iron that breaketh all these, shall it break in pieces and bruise. And whereas thou sawest the feet and toes, part of potters' clay, and part of iron, the kingdom shall be divided; but there shall be in it of the strength of the iron, forasmuch as thou sawest the iron mixed with miry clay. And as the toes of the feet were part of iron, and part of clay, so the kingdom shall be partly strong, and partly broken. And whereas thou sawest iron mixed with miry clay, they shall mingle themselves with the seed of men: but they shall not cleave one to another, even as iron is not mixed with clay. And in the days of these kings shall the God of heaven set up a kingdom, which shall never be destroyed: and the kingdom shall not be left to other people, but it shall break in pieces and consume all these kingdoms, and it shall stand for ever. Forasmuch as thou sawest that the stone was cut out of the**	**"But Jesus beheld them, and said unto them, With men this is impossible; but with God all things are possible"** (Mt.19:26). **"Now to him that is of power to stablish you according to my gospel, and the preaching of Jesus Christ, according to the revelation of the mystery, which was kept secret since the world began"** (Ro.16:25). **"For I lift up my hand to heaven, and say, I live for ever"** (De.32:40). **"The eternal God is thy refuge, and underneath are the everlasting arms"** (De.33:27). **"Thy name, O LORD, endureth for ever; and thy memorial, O Lord, throughout all generations"** (Ps.135:13). **"I am Alpha and Omega, the beginning and the ending, saith the Lord, which is, and which was, and which is to come, the Almighty"** (Re.1:8). **"Thine, O LORD, is the greatness, and the power, and the glory, and the victory, and the majesty: for all that is in the heav-en and in the earth is thine; thine is the kingdom, O LORD, and thou art exalted as head above all"** (1 Chr.29:11). **"The LORD reigneth, he is clothed with majesty; the LORD is clothed with strength, wherewith he hath girded himself: the world also is stablished, that it cannot be moved"** (Ps.93:1). **"I will speak of the glorious honour of thy majesty, and of thy wondrous works"** (Ps.145:5). **"And the seventh angel sounded; and there were great voices in heaven, saying, The kingdoms of this world are become the kingdoms of our Lord, and of his Christ; and he shall reign for ever and ever"** (Re.11:15).

PROPHET	TIME/PLACE GIVEN	MAIN MESSAGE	PRACTICAL APPLICATION
DANIEL (cont.) 12. The vision of the man dressed in linen standing by the Tigris River (Da.10:1-14). 13. The vision of the man who strengthened Daniel (Da.10:15-21). 14. The prophecy about the coming Greek Empire and Alexander the Great (Da.11:2-4). 15. The prophecies about the coming empires of Egypt and Syria and their struggle for world power (Da.11:5-35). 16. The prophecy of the distressing time at the end of the world—that those whose names are written in the Book of Life will be rescued (Da.12:1). 17. The prophecy of additional resurrections during the Tribulation (Da.12:2-3). **Scripture References** The book of *Daniel*		mountain without hands, and that it brake in pieces the iron, the brass, the clay, the silver, and the gold; the great God hath made known to the king what shall come to pass hereafter: and the dream is certain, and the interpretation thereof sure" (Da.2:36-45). "How great are his signs! and how mighty are his wonders! his kingdom is an everlasting kingdom, and his dominion is from generation to generation" (Da. 4:3). "And at the end of the days I Nebuchadnezzar lifted up mine eyes unto heaven, and mine understanding returned unto me, and I blessed the most High, and I praised and honoured him that liveth for ever, whose dominion is an everlasting dominion, and his kingdom is from generation to generation: And all the inhabitants of the earth are reputed as nothing: and he doeth according to his will in the army of heaven, and among the inhabitants of the earth: and none can stay his hand, or say unto him, What doest thou?" (Da.4:34-35). "And this is the writing that was written, MENE, MENE, TEKEL, UPHARSIN. This is the interpretation of the thing: MENE; God hath numbered thy kingdom, and finished it. TEKEL; Thou art weighed in the balances, and art found wanting. PERES; Thy kingdom is divided, and given to the Medes and Persians" (Da.5:25-28).	

PROPHET	TIME/PLACE GIVEN	MAIN MESSAGE	PRACTICAL APPLICATION
## DAVID (Loved) **Known Facts** 1. Was the son of Jesse and the youngest of eight sons (1 S.16:11; 17:12). 2. Lived in Bethlehem (1 S.16:1; 17:12). 3. Descended from the tribe of Judah (Mt. 1:1-6). 4. Served the first king of Israel, King Saul, by playing music for him and by serving in Saul's army (1 S.16:23; 18:5). 5. Defeated the giant Goliath as a youth (1 S.17). 6. Was anointed king over all Israel and reigned forty years (1 S.16:1, 11-13; 2 S.5:5). 7. Was promised by God that the Savior would come through his lineage (Mt.1:1-17). 8. Wrote 73 Psalms (Ps. 22:1; 23:1; 41:1; 110:1). 9. Played musical instruments in praise to the LORD (2 S.23:2). 10. Was a brilliant military leader and strategist. Led great military campaigns (1 S. 18:5-7). 11. Had a heart that was like the heart of God (1 S.13:14; Ac.13:22). **Predictions and Messages** 1. The Messiah, the Savior of the world, would be a priest after the order of Melchizedek (Ps.110:4; Mt. 27:50-51; Mk. 15:37-38; Lu.23:44-46; He.6:20). 2. The Messiah would be betrayed by a friend (Ps.41:9; Mt. 26:20-25; Mk.14:10-11; Lu.22:2-6; Jn. 13:1-2; 1 Co.11:23). 3. The Messiah's betrayer would be removed from office and replaced (Ps. 109:7-8; Ac.1:18-20). (Cont. on next page)	**Time** *1029–971 B.C. All his life, King David sang and wrote psalms (songs) to the LORD. In his times of rejoicing and in his time of despair, David cried out to God in beautiful songs of poetry.* **Place** *Many places throughout Judea and Samaria as well as southern Jerusalem, the City of David.*	David was a shining example of trust in God, of placing his life in the palm of God's hand. Whenever David was in trouble, he turned to God as His Savior, trusting the LORD completely for deliverance. And the LORD always saved, delivered David because of the saving acts of God and in his behalf, David was able to write many heartfelt Psalms that are recorded in the Holy Scripture. And God was able to use David to predict many of the prophecies about Jesus Christ hundreds of years before the Savior was born. **"Now these are the last words of David. David the son of Jesse declares, The man who was raised on high declares, The anointed of the God of Jacob, And the sweet psalmist of Israel, 'The Spirit of the Lord spoke by me, And His word was on my tongue'" (2 S.23:1-2).**	David trusted fully that God would do exactly as He had promised, that He would send the promised King and Savior to establish His throne forever in the world. The confessions of David's heart were made in simple trust, arising from a heart that was truly convinced that God does exactly what He says He will do. David's trust is a dynamic example for us, for it is simple trust God desires from man—nothing more and nothing less. We simply must rely on God. We must lean on Him with our whole heart, put our complete trust in the LORD to do exactly as He says. The LORD will save those who trust in Him. **"The God of my rock; in him will I trust: he is my shield, and the horn of my salvation, my high tower, and my refuge, my saviour; thou savest me from violence" (2 S.22:3).** **"But let all those that put their trust in thee rejoice: let them ever shout for joy, because thou defendest them: let them also that love thy name be joyful in thee" (Ps.5:11).** **"O LORD my God, in thee do I put my trust: save me from all them that persecute me, and deliver me" (Ps.7:1).** **"The LORD redeemeth the soul of his servants: and none of them that trust in him shall be desolate" (Ps.34:22).** **"Cause me to hear thy lovingkindness in the morning; for in thee do I trust: cause me to know the way wherein I should walk; for I lift up my soul unto thee" (Ps.143:8).**

PROPHET	TIME/PLACE GIVEN	MAIN MESSAGE	PRACTICAL APPLICATION
DAVID (cont.) 4. The Messiah, the Savior of the world, would be falsely accused (Ps. 27:12; 35:11; Mt. 26:59-62; Mk. 14:55-59). 5. The Messiah would be hated for no reason (Ps.69:4; Jn.15:23-25). 6. The Messiah's hands and feet would be pierced (Ps.22:16; Jn. 20:25-27). 7. The Messiah would bear the sins of the world (Ps.22:1; Mt. 27:45-46; Mk.15:33-34). 8. The Messiah would be mocked (Ps.22:6-8; Mt.27:39-40; Mk. 15:29-32; Lu. 23:35-37). 9. The Messiah would be given gall and vinegar (Ps.69:21; Mt. 27:48; Mk.15:36; Jn. 19:28-29). 10. The Messiah would pray for His enemies (Ps.109:4; Lu.23:34). 11. The Messiah's garments would be gambled for (Ps.22:18; Mt.27:35; Mk.15:24; Lu.23:34; Jn.19:23-25). 12. The Messiah would not have any broken bones (Ps.34:20; see Ex. 12:46; Jn.19:31-37). 13. The Messiah would be resurrected (Ps. 16:10; Mt.12:39-41; 16:4; 28:1-7; Mk. 16:1-8; Lu.11:29-32; 24:1-8; Jn.20:1-8). 14. The Messiah would ascend to heaven (Ps. 68:18; Mk.16:19-20; Lu.24:50-51; Ac.1:6-9; Ep.4:8-10). **Scripture References** 1 S.16–1 K. 2; Ps.16, 22, 27, 34, 41, 68, 69, 109, 110			

THE PROPHETS

PROPHET	TIME/PLACE GIVEN	MAIN MESSAGE	PRACTICAL APPLICATION
DEBORAH (Honey bee) **Known Facts** 1. Was married to Lapidoth (Jud.4:4). 2. Judged Israel, deciding civil cases for the people according to God's Word (Jud. 4:4). 3. Wrote a song of deliverance after the defeat of Sisera and the Canaanite army (Jud.5). **Predictions and Messages** 1. Barak was to gather ten thousand men from Naphtali and Zebulun, and God would deliver Sisera into his hand (Jud.4:4-8). 2. Sisera would be killed by a woman because Barak refused to go without Deborah (Jud.4:9). **Scripture References** Jud.4-5	**Time** *Approximately 1220 B.C., during a time of oppression by King Jabin of the Canaanites. It was about 200 plus years before King David and about 200 plus after the Exodus.* **Place** *Between Ramah and Bethel, in the hill country of Ephraim.*	The LORD is a mighty Deliverer, Who will deliver Israel from the Canaanite enemies. Through Deborah, God instructed Barak to mobilize ten thousand troops and to meet the enemy commander Sisera, at the Kishon River. Gripped by fear and feeling inadequate for the task, Barak refused to go without Deborah's help. Granting his request, God used both Deborah and Barak to soundly defeat the oppressing Canaanites in a tremendous victory. But because Barak refused to obey God, he was denied the honor of capturing the enemy commander Sisera. Instead, the honor of killing the dreaded enemy commander was given to a woman name Jael. **"Now she sent and summoned Barak the son of Abinoam from Kedesh-naphtali, and said to him, 'Behold, the LORD, the God of Israel, has commanded, "Go and march to Mount Tabor, and take with you ten thousand men from the sons of Naphtali and from the sons of Zebulun. I will draw out to you Sisera, the commander of Jabin's army, with his chariots and his many troops to the river Kishon, and I will give him into your hand."' Then Barak said to her, 'If you will go with me, then I will go; but if you will not go with me, I will not go.' She said, 'I will surely go with you; nevertheless, the honor shall not be yours on the journey that you are about to take, for the LORD will sell Sisera into the hands of a woman.' Then Deborah arose and went with Barak to Kedesh" (Jud.4:6-9).**	The courage of Deborah stands as a dynamic example for us all. Just imagine—facing a massive army unarmed! Deborah courageously accepted this challenge, but not Barak. He was reluctant, fainthearted, fearful, and unbelieving. From this experience of Deborah and Barak, we must learn one lesson: there is no room in the service of God for being fainthearted, fearful, or unbelieving. God commands us to be courageous, to step forth and face the enemy with courage and boldness, No matter what the enemy or its power, we are to be courageous in standing against it. God promises to help us and to deliver us if we will confront the enemy courageously in His name. **"Have I not commanded thee? Be strong and of a good courage; be not afraid, neither be thou dismayed: for the LORD thy God is with thee whithersoever thou goest" (Jos.1:9).** **"The wicked flee when no man pursueth, But the righteous are bold as a lion" (Pr.28:1).** **"Fear thou not; for I am with thee: be not dismayed; for I am thy God: I will strengthen thee; yea, I will help thee; yea, I will uphold thee with the right hand of my righteousness" (Is.41:10).**

PROPHET	TIME/PLACE GIVEN	MAIN MESSAGE	PRACTICAL APPLICATION
ELIEZER (God is my Helper) **Known Facts** 1. Was the son of Dodavah (2 Chr. 20:37). 2. Lived in Mareshah (2 Chr.20:37). **Predictions and Messages** Rebuked King Jehoshaphat for forming an alliance with an evil king, King Ahaziah of the Northern Kingdom of Israel (2 Chr.20:37). **Scripture References** 2 Chr.20:35-37	**Time** *849-48 B.C., at the end of the reign of Jehoshaphat, king of Judah.* **Place** *Jerusalem, the capital of the Southern Kingdom of Judah.*	Eliezer rebuked King Jehoshaphat of Judah for making an agreement with the evil King Ahaziah of the Northern Kingdom of Israel. Eliezer declared that God had caused their gold-seeking ships to be destroyed because God was so displeased with Jehoshaphat's actions. **"And after this did Jehoshaphat king of Judah join himself with Ahaziah king of Israel, who did very wickedly: And he joined himself with him to make ships to go to Tarshish: and they made the ships in Eziongeber. Then Eliezer the son of Dodavah of Mareshah prophesied against Jehoshaphat, saying, Because thou hast joined thyself with Aha-ziah, the LORD hath broken thy works. And the ships were broken, that they were not able to go to Tarshish" (2 Chr.20:35-37).**	God warns the believer against compromising and forming worldly alliances with the unbelievers and wicked people of this world. God demands spiritual separation. For if we fellowship, closely associate with the sinful and wicked of this earth, eventually we will be seduced to join in and participate in their sin. Compromise is forbidden by God. We are to live lives of spiritual separation, not compromising our commitment to God, not engaging in the sinful and wicked behavior of unbelievers. **"And take heed to yourselves, lest at any time your hearts be overcharged with surfeiting, and drunkenness, and cares of this life, and so that day come upon you unawares" (Lu.21:34).** **"I beseech you therefore, brethren, by the mercies of God, that ye present your bodies a living sacrifice, holy, acceptable unto God, which is your reasonable service. And be not conformed to this world: but be ye transformed by the renewing of your mind, that ye may prove what is that good, and acceptable, and perfect, will of God" (Ro.12:1-2).** **"But now I have written unto you not to keep company, if any man that is called a brother be a fornicator, or covetous, or an idolater, or a railer, or a drunkard, or an extortioner; with such an one no not to eat" (1 Co.5:11).**

PROPHET	TIME/PLACE GIVEN	MAIN MESSAGE	PRACTICAL APPLICATION
ELIJAH (Yahweh is God) **Known Facts** 1. Was from Tishbi (1 K.17:1). 2. Lived in Gilead (1 K.17:1). 3. Ministered to the Northern Kingdom of Israel (1 K.17:1). 4. Performed many miracles: ➤ Prevented rain for three years (1 K.17:1; Js.5:17). ➤ Multiplied flour and oil during the entire time of the drought (1 K.17:14). ➤ Raised a child from the dead (1 K.17:22). ➤ Called fire down from heaven (1 K.18:38; 2 K.1:10). ➤ Brought rain (1 K.18:41). ➤ Divided the Jordan River and crossed on dry ground (2 K.2:8). **Predictions and Messages** 1. A long, severe drought would come to Israel (1 K.17:1). 2. The flour and oil of the widow of Zarepath would multiply miraculously so that she would have an unending daily supply as long as the drought continued (1 K.17:14). 3. A torrential rain would come to end the long drought (1 K.18:41). 4. The blood of Ahab would be licked up by the dogs to avenge the blood of Naboth (1 K. 21:19; 2 K.9:24-26). 5. The household of Ahab would be destroyed and come to a complete end (1 K.21:21-24). **Scripture References** 1 K.17–2 K.2	**Time** *860-845 B.C., during the reigns of Ahab, Ahaziah, and Jehoram, kings of Northern Israel.* **Place** *The Northern Kingdom of Israel.*	For over three years, Elijah predicted that it would not rain. Through this terrible drought, Elijah was able to warn the people time and again against the false worship of Baal. Baal was thought to be the god of the weather and fertility, and the worship of this false god was strongly encouraged by King Ahab and Queen Jezebel. But with fervor and stunning miracles, God called people to repentance through Elijah's ministry. Finally, a showdown was held between Elijah and the false prophets of Baal, a confrontation that was to prove once and for all who the real God was. Perhaps no scene in the Old Testament is more dramatic than when Elijah called down fire from heaven upon his sacrifice on Mt. Carmel. The spectacular, miraculous event proved once for all that Jehovah/Yahweh is the One True God, the only real and living God. Sadly, despite this tremendous display of God's power, Ahab and the people still did not repent. **"And Elijah the Tishbite, who was of the inhabitants of Gilead, said unto Ahab, As the Lord God of Israel liveth, before whom I stand, there shall not be dew nor rain these years, but according to my word" (1 K.17:1).** **"For thus saith the Lord God of Israel, The barrel of meal shall not waste, neither shall the cruse of oil fail, until the day that the Lord sendeth rain upon the earth" (1 K.17:14).** **"And Elijah said unto Ahab, Get thee up, eat and drink; for there is a sound of abundance of rain" (1 K.18:41).** **"And will make thine house like the house of Jeroboam the son of Nebat, and like the house of Baasha the son of Ahijah, for the provocation wherewith thou hast provoked me to anger, and made Israel to sin" (1 K.21:22).**	1. The LORD (Jehovah, Yahweh) is the One and only living and true God: there is no other God. All false gods are just this: false. They are nonexistent, not really living, not possessing life. They are powerless, unable to respond. Being lifeless, they cannot hear prayers, nor reach out to help us in our desperate hours of need. False gods are totally incapable of being present with us as we walk day by day. They are unable to guide us or to fulfill any promise ever made by a false prophet. All other so-called gods are false. They exist only in a person's imagination. 2. If a person refuses to believe God's Word, he will not believe nor follow the Lord, even if he sees a dramatic sign from heaven. **"I am Alpha and Omega, the beginning and the ending, saith the Lord, which is, and which was, and which is to come, the Almighty" (Re.1:8).** **"Fear ye not, neither be afraid: have not I told thee from that time, and have declared it? ye are even my witnesses. Is there a God beside me? yea, there is no God; I know not any" (Is.44:8).** **"Then the steward said within himself, What shall I do? for my lord taketh away from me the stewardship: I cannot dig; to beg I am ashamed" (Lu.16:31).**

PROPHET	TIME/PLACE GIVEN	MAIN MESSAGE	PRACTICAL APPLICATION

ELISHA
(God is the Savior)
 	
Known Facts
1. Was the son of Shaphat (1 K.19:16).
2. Lived in Abel-Meholah (1 K.19:16).
3. Was anointed by Elijah to take his place, as God instructed (1 K.19:16).
4. Performed many miracles:
  ➤ Parted the Jordan River (2 K.2:14).
  ➤ Made bitter water sweet (2 K.2:19-22).
  ➤ Saved an army by causing water to appear in ditches (2 K.3:13-20).
  ➤ Multiplied the widow's oil (2 K.4:1-7).
  ➤ Raised a child from the dead (2 K.4:32-37).
  ➤ Purified a pot of food from poison (2 K.4:38-41).
  ➤ Multiplied bread and grain to feed one hundred men (2 K.4:42-44).
  ➤ Healed a leper (2 K.5:1-14).
  ➤ Caused an ax head to float in the Jordan River (2 K.6:1-7).
  ➤ Raised a man from the dead, when the man came in contact with Elisha's bones (2 K.13:21).
5. Prophesied in the Northern Kingdom (2 K. 2:2).
6. Saw Elijah transported to heaven (2 K.2:9-13).
7. Was the model of a spiritual leader (1 K. 19:19-21; 2 K.5:16).
 	
(Cont. on next page)
	Time
	850–795 B.C., during the reigns of Jehoram, Jehu, Jehoahaz, and Jehoash, kings of Northern Israel.
	
	Place
	Israel, The Northern Kingdom of Israel.
		God will save those who have faith in Him. Time and time again, in both the words and deeds of Elisha, this message of salvation was demonstrated.
		
		Elisha had strong faith in God and faithfully followed God. But he not only followed, he demonstrated an iron determination in living a godly, righteous life. Elisha's life was a beacon, a bright example to everyone he met. Persevering to his very last day on earth, he repeatedly demonstrated the saving, miraculous power of God.
		
		"And he went forth unto the spring of the waters, and cast the salt in there, and said, Thus saith the LORD, I have healed these waters; there shall not be from thence any more death or barren land" (2 K.2:21).
		"For thus saith the LORD, Ye shall not see wind, neither shall ye see rain; yet that valley shall be filled with water, that ye may drink, both ye, and your cattle, and your beasts" (2 K.3:17).
		"And his servitor said, What, should I set this before an hundred men? He said again, Give the people, that they may eat: for thus saith the LORD, They shall eat, and shall leave thereof" (2 K.4:43).
		"And he said unto him, Went not mine heart with thee, when the man turned again from his chariot to meet thee? Is it a time to receive money, and to receive garments, and oliveyards, and vineyards, and sheep, and oxen, and menservants, and maidservants? The leprosy therefore of Naaman shall cleave unto thee, and unto thy seed for ever. And he went out from his presence a leper as white as snow" (2 K.5:26-27).
		"Then Elisha said, Hear ye the word of the LORD; Thus saith the LORD, To morrow about this time shall a measure of fine flour be sold for a shekel, and two measures of barley for a shekel, in the gate of Samaria. Then a lord on whose hand the king leaned answered the man of God, and said, Behold, if the LORD would make windows in heaven, might this thing be? And
			Far too often men and women demonstrate traits of weak character, traits such as insincerity, deception, impurity, dishonesty, corruption and wickedness. Whereas they should be living lives of honor, goodness, purity, morality, and sincerity. This is not the way any of us should be living. We should be men and women of honor and uprightness, holding ever so high the principles of morality, righteousness and justice for all people everywhere.
			
			We should be followers of Christ, and we should persevere, be steadfast in our faith. Once we profess Christ, we must continue to profess and follow after Him. *Continuing on* is the evidence of our faith. When people see us continuing to follow Christ, they know that our profession is true. But if we profess to be a follower of the LORD and then refuse to live like He says, people know that we are making a false profession. We must *continue on,* being steadfast, enduring, persevering in following Christ—this assures our salvation, that our profession is true, that our life demonstrates what we say.
			
			"Awake to righteousness, and sin not; for some have not the knowledge of God: I speak this to your shame" (1 Co.15:34).
			"Knowing that whatsoever good thing any man doeth, the same shall he receive of the Lord, whether he be bond or free" (Ep.6:8).
			"But thou, O man of God, flee these things; and follow after righteousness, godliness, faith, love, patience, meekness. Fight the good fight of faith, lay hold on eternal life, whereunto thou art also called, and hast professed a good profession before many witnesses" (1 Ti.6:11-12).
			"Teaching us that, denying ungodliness and worldly lusts, we should live soberly, righteously, and godly, in this present world; Looking for that blessed hope, and the glorious appearing of the great God and our Saviour Jesus Christ" (Tit.2:12-13).
			"And ye shall serve the Lord your God, and he shall bless thy bread, and thy water; and I will take sickness away from the midst of thee" (Ex.23:25).

PROPHET	TIME/PLACE GIVEN	MAIN MESSAGE	PRACTICAL APPLICATION
ELISHA (cont.) **Predictions and Messages** 1. The water of a spring would be purified, will be sweet (2 K. 2:21). 2. Water would miraculously appear in some trenches especially prepared by faith to catch the water (2 K.3:17). 3. Food would be multiplied (2 K.4:43). 4. Gehazi and his descendants would be struck with leprosy (2 K.5:26-27). 5. A great famine would end in one day (2 K.7:1). 6. The king's attendant would see the end of the famine, but would not eat any of the food because he did not believe the Word of the LORD (2 K. 7:2). 7. Jehu would become king and kill the entire family of Ahab (2 K.9:6-8). 8. The prediction that Israel would have three victories over Syria (2 K.13:14-19). **Scripture References** 1 K.19:16-19; 2 K.2–13		he said, Behold, thou shalt see it with thine eyes, but shalt not eat thereof" (2 K.7:1-2). "And he arose, and went into the house; and he poured the oil on his head, and said unto him, Thus saith the LORD God of Israel, I have anointed thee king over the people of the Lord, even over Israel. And thou shalt smite the house of Ahab thy master, that I may avenge the blood of my servants the prophets, and the blood of all the servants of the LORD, at the hand of Jezebel. For the whole house of Ahab shall perish: and I will cut off from Ahab him that pisseth against the wall, and him that is shut up and left in Israel" (2 K.9:6-8).	"He withdraweth not his eyes from the righteous: but with kings are they on the throne; yea, he doth establish them for ever, and they are exalted" (Jb.36:7). "The eyes of the Lord are upon the righteous, and his ears are open unto their cry" (Ps.34:15). "I have been young, and now am old; yet have I not seen the righteous forsaken, nor his seed begging bread" (Ps.37:25).

PROPHET	TIME/PLACE GIVEN	MAIN MESSAGE	PRACTICAL APPLICATION
EZEKIEL (God is strong) **Known Facts** 1. Was the son of Buzi (Eze.1:3). 2. Served as a priest in the temple (Eze.1:3). 3. Wrote the book of *Ezekiel* (Eze.1:1-3). 4. Was taken captive into Babylon (Eze. 1:2; 2 K.24:11-16). 5. Called to be a watchman to the people of Israel (Eze. 3:17). 6. Called to be a sign or symbol to the people of Israel (Eze.12:6, 11; 24:21-27). **Predictions and Messages** 1. Visions of the glory of the LORD and Ezekiel's calling (Eze.1–3). 2. Prophecies concerning Judah and Jerusalem—that God would judge and send the people into captivity because they profaned the holy temple (Eze.4–24). 3. Prophecies concerning other nations—that God would judge their sin, especially Egypt, but Israel will be restored (Eze.25–32). 4. Prophecies concerning the restoring of Israel—that Israel would be restored when the people repented and turned back to the LORD (Eze.33–39). 5. A vision and a detailed description of the future temple and of heaven (Eze.40–48). **Scripture References** The book of *Ezekiel*	**Time** *593–571 B.C., before and during the final captivity and exile of Judah and Jerusalem in 586 B.C.* **Place** *Ezekiel first prophesied in Jerusalem, but later was taken captive into Babylon. In Babylon (or the land of the Chaldeans), Ezekiel was sitting next to the River Chebar when the Spirit of God revealed to him strange and wonderful visions of the glory of the LORD and of heaven (Eze.1:3).*	"Know that I am the LORD." This main message of Ezekiel occurs sixty-three times throughout the book of *Ezekiel*. Ezekiel's messages strongly emphasized the holiness of God, and the fact that God will judge sin. But the LORD will also forgive and restore those who repent and turn to Him. God is known by His judgment; but He is better known by His mercy. Throughout his ministry, Ezekiel was greatly persecuted and eventually killed for his straightforward preaching. But he stood fast, unswervingly preaching the messages the LORD laid upon his heart. **"For every one of the house of Israel, or of the stranger that sojourneth in Israel, which separateth himself from me, and setteth up his idols in his heart, and putteth the stumblingblock of his iniquity before his face, and cometh to a prophet to enquire of him concerning me; I the LORD will answer him by myself: And I will set my face against that man, and will make him a sign and a proverb, and I will cut him off from the midst of my people; and ye shall know that I am the LORD" (Eze.14:7-8).** **"And they shall know that I am the LORD, and that I have not said in vain that I would do this evil unto them" (Eze.6:10).** **"But if the wicked will turn from all his sins that he hath committed, and keep all my statutes, and do that which is lawful and right, he shall surely live, he shall not die" (Eze.18:21).** **"Say unto them, As I live, saith the Lord GOD, I have no pleasure in the death of the wicked; but that the wicked turn from his way and live: turn ye, turn ye from your evil ways; for why will ye die?" (Eze.33:11).**	Despite the love of God, people shockingly reject the LORD. This is why God judges and shows His wrath. Man is without excuse. Man has no defense, no answer, no reason that can justify his rebellion against God. Yet God is merciful to the person who repents. He gave His Son to die for us. We do not deserve it—we never have and we never will—but God loves us with an incomprehensible love. Therefore, He has given His Son to die *for* us, as our substitute, in our behalf. But a person must accept the gift of God's Son, accept Jesus Christ by true faith and repentance in order to receive God's mercy. **"Let the wicked forsake his way, and the unrighteous man his thoughts: and let him return unto the LORD, and he will have mercy upon him; and to our God, for he will abundantly pardon" (Is.55:7).** **"Therefore say thou unto them, Thus saith the LORD of hosts; Turn ye unto me, saith the LORD of hosts, and I will turn unto you, saith the LORD of hosts" (Zec. 1:3).**

PROPHET	TIME/PLACE GIVEN	MAIN MESSAGE	PRACTICAL APPLICATION
GAD (Fortunate) **Known Facts** 1. Recorded some of the history of King David (1 Chr.29:29-30). 2. Ministered as a prophet for many years. 3. Served by the side of King David and King Solomon as the king's seer (2 Chr.29:25). **Predictions and Messages** 1. Warned David to flee from Judah whenever Saul was about to find him (1 S.22:5). 2. Announced God's judgment for David's sin of numbering the people (2 S.24:10-15; 1 Chr.21:9-13). 3. Gave instructions to David for ending the severe plague of judgment on the people (2 S. 24:18-19; 1 Chr. 21:18-19). **Scripture References** 1 S.22:4; 2 S.24:11-19; 1 Chr.9-19; 2 Chr.29:25	**Time** *1015–950 B.C., before the division of the nation of Israel.* **Place** *Jerusalem and certain areas to the south, while he served by the side of King David and King Solomon.*	Our strength and security is in the LORD. No amount of human ability or might can keep us safe—only God can. So as we face the trials, temptations and enemies of life, we must remain humble before the LORD, never allowing ourselves to become puffed up with pride, thinking that we have some great ability or resource to conquer the hardships and sufferings of life. It is never by our own strength, but God's that we triumph in life. **"They dwelt with him all the while that David was in the hold. And the prophet Gad said unto David, Abide not in the hold; depart, and get thee into the land of Judah. Then David departed, and came into the forest of Hareth" (1 S.22:4-5).** **"The word of the LORD came unto the prophet Gad, David's seer, saying, Go and say unto David, Thus saith the LORD, I offer thee three things; choose thee one of them, that I may do it unto thee. So Gad came to David, and told him, and said unto him, Shall seven years of famine come unto thee in thy land? or wilt thou flee three months before thine enemies, while they pursue thee? or that there be three days' pestilence in thy land?...advise, and see what answer I shall return to him that sent me" (2 S.24:11-13).** **"Then the angel of the LORD commanded Gad to say to David, that David should go up, and set up an altar unto the LORD in the threshingfloor of Ornan the Jebusite. And David went up at the saying of Gad, which he spake in the name of the LORD....Then David said to Ornan, Grant me...this threshingfloor, that I may build an altar...unto the LORD:...that the plague may be stayed from the people" And David built there an altar unto the LORD, and offered burnt offerings and peace offerings, and called upon the LORD; and he answered him from heaven by fire upon the altar of burnt offering. And the LORD commanded the angel; and he put up his sword again into the sheath thereof" (1 Chr.21:18-19, 22, 26-27).**	A spirit of pride, conceit, and haughtiness is a terrible evil. For when we exalt ourselves, we walk around acting as though we are better, more capable, more deserving, more moral, more righteous than someone else. But note this inescapable truth: we reap what we sow. If we sow prideful sin and evil, we reap the consequences. So it is with any act of wickedness. This is a spiritual law set up by God for the purpose of divine judgment. A person may repent, but the wickedness will result in some consequence of suffering. **"Pride goeth before destruction, and an haughty spirit before a fall" (Pr.16:18).** **"Be not deceived; God is not mocked: for whatsoever a man soweth, that shall he also reap" (Ga.6:7).** **"With him is an arm of flesh; but with us is the LORD our God to help us, and to fight our battles" (2 Chr.32:8).** **"He that trusteth in his own heart is a fool: but whoso walketh wisely, he shall be delivered" (Pr.28:26).**

PROPHET	TIME/PLACE GIVEN	MAIN MESSAGE	PRACTICAL APPLICATION

HABAKKUK (Tightly embraced)
 	
Known Facts
1. Ministered to Judah, the Southern Kingdom.
2. Wrote the book of *Habakkuk* (Hab.1:1).
 	
Predictions and Messages
1. The oracle of the wickedness of the people (Hab.1:1-4).
2. The oracle of the shocking invasion of the Chaldeans (Hab. 1:5-17).
3. The answer of God to Habakkuk's plea—the wicked will be judged, but the righteous will live by faith (Hab.2:1-20).
4. The prayer of Habakkuk—the LORD is glorious and mighty (Hab.3:1-16).
5. The praise of Habakkuk—the LORD protects those who trust in Him even in the midst of trouble and distress (Hab.3:17-20).
 	
Scripture References
The book of *Habakkuk*; Ro.1:17; Ga.3:11-12; He.10:37-38
	Time
	615-598 B.C., during the reigns of Jehoahaz and Jehoiakim, about 20 years before the captivity of Judah and Jerusalem.
	
	Place
	Judah, the Southern Kingdom.
		The heart of Habakkuk ached to the point of breaking. The prophet was in anguish for three reasons. First, Habakkuk saw the horrible wickedness of Israel, the deep sin of his own people. Second, he knew that the terrible judgment of God's hand was coming because of Israel's sin. Third, and what weighed most heavily on his soul, Habakkuk longed to be acceptable before the holy God Whom he served.
		    In his book, Habakkuk recorded several question he asked of God and the LORD's answer to his questions. After humbly pleading and lamenting to the LORD, Habakkuk waited (for the prophet never presumed, not even for a moment, that God is unjust). He simply asked his questions and then waited for the LORD to change his heart, so that he could fully trust Him.
		    Among the LORD's answer to Habakkuk is the vital message found in Hab.2:4. This important verse teaches us that we must guard against pride and trust in God. Habakkuk faithfully preached this message, longing for his people to listen and repent.
		
		    "Therefore the law is slacked, and judgment doth never go forth: for the wicked doth compass about the righteous; therefore wrong judgment proceedeth" (Hab.1:4).
		    "For, lo, I raise up the Chaldeans, that bitter and hasty nation, which shall march through the breadth of the land, to possess the dwellingplaces that are not theirs" (Hab.1:6).
		    "Behold, his soul which is lifted up is not upright in him: but the just shall live by his faith" (Hab.2:4).
		    "God came from Teman, and the Holy One from mount Paran. Selah. His glory covered the heavens, and the earth was full of his praise" (Hab.3:3).
		    "The LORD God is my strength, and he will make my feet like hinds' feet, and he will make me to walk upon mine high places" (Hab.3:19).
			God's chosen way for us to approach Him is that we "live by faith." After all, Scripture declares as clearly as it can: no man is justified by the law in the sight of God. God is perfect; He is perfectly righteous. No man can achieve perfection; therefore, no man can live in the presence of God. No matter how good he is or how much good he does, he cannot achieve perfection. The fact is evident, for if a man had achieved perfection, he would be perfect—living forever in a perfect state of being, even on this earth.
			    But note this: What God does is take a person's faith and count that faith as righteousness, as perfection. Therefore, a man is able to live in God's presence by faith or justification. The point is this: God's way for a man to approach Him is the way of faith: "The just shall live by faith."
			
			    "But without faith it is impossible to please him: for he that cometh to God must believe that he is, and that he is a rewarder of them that diligently seek him" (He.11:6).
			    "Let the heavens be glad, and let the earth rejoice: and let men say among the nations, The LORD reigneth" (1 Chr.16:31).
			    "God reigneth over the heathen: God sitteth upon the throne of his holiness" (Ps.47:8).
			    "Let not thine heart envy sinners: but be thou in the fear of the LORD all the day long" (Pr.23:17).
			    "I know that, whatsoever God doeth, it shall be for ever: nothing can be put to it, nor any thing taken from it: and God doeth it, that men should fear before him" (Ec.3:14).

PROPHET	TIME/PLACE GIVEN	MAIN MESSAGE	PRACTICAL APPLICATION
HAGGAI **(Feast of Yahweh)** **Known Facts** 1. Ministered to Judah, the Southern Kingdom. 2. Wrote the book of *Haggai* (Hag.1:1). **Predictions and Messages** 1. The declaration that it is time to build the temple of the LORD (Hag.1:2). 2. A sermon about taking courage because the LORD is with you (Hag.2:4). 3. The foretelling of the future blessing of Israel by the LORD (Hag.2:19). 4. The prophecy that Zerubbabel will be lifted up as a leader (Hag.2:23). **Scripture References** The book of *Haggai*; Ezr.5:1; 6:14	**Time** *520 B.C., when the second foundation of the temple was to be laid.* **Place** *Jerusalem, the Holy City and place of the temple.*	Haggai's messages were given to encourage and strengthen the returned exiles of Jerusalem as they sought to rebuild their temple and nation. He taught that the Spirit of the LORD mightily dwells among those who reverence and honor Him. The citizens of Jerusalem at this time had just returned from captivity in Babylon. Although they were in their own land, it was new and unfamiliar because it was their ancestors, not them, who had been taken captive seventy years before. Naturally, the people were glad to be free. But they still felt somewhat discouraged, unsure of what to do next. They were a people without direction. Through the prophet Haggai, the LORD gave special direction and greatly encouraged the people. Haggai told of a bright future and promised a strong leader in Zerubbabel. Most of all, the Spirit of the LORD would be among the people if they would honor the LORD and give Him their true heartfelt worship. **"Thus speaketh the LORD of hosts, saying, This people say, The time is not come, the time that the LORD's house should be built" (Hag.1:2).** **"Yet now be strong, O Zerubbabel, saith the LORD; and be strong, O Joshua, son of Josedech, the high priest; and be strong, all ye people of the land, saith the LORD, and work: for I am with you, saith the LORD of hosts" (Hag.2:4).** **"Is the seed yet in the barn? yea, as yet the vine, and the fig tree, and the pomegranate, and the olive tree, hath not brought forth: from this day will I bless you" (Hag.2:19).** **"In that day, saith the LORD of hosts, will I take thee, O Zerubbabel, my servant, the son of Shealtiel, saith the LORD, and will make thee as a signet: for I have chosen thee, saith the LORD of hosts" (Hag.2:23).**	How many of us have little rituals, prayers, habits, ceremonies, and objects that we use to keep us religiously secure? So many of us seek religious security while at the same time we neglect the weightier matter of breaking God's Law. It is not the man-made place or the man-made ritual that saves a person. What saves a person is coming to God in true worship, bowing before Him, acknowledging Him as God, acknowledging that His Son, Jesus Christ, is the only way and the only hope of salvation. The place of worship is no longer the temple or any other particular location on earth. God's presence now dwells in the hearts and lives of His people. His people worship Him wherever they are, and they can worship Him every day all day long. True worship means that we focus on the object of worship, being sure that we are truly worshipping the Father, God Himself. A person may be in a fancy, expensive church or in a broom closet worshipping, and yet not be worshipping the Father. A man's whole being must be focused upon the only true and living God, worshipping Him and Him alone. God desires worship, for He created man to worship and fellowship with Him. Therefore, man needs to truly worship God. Man needs to worship God with the spiritual drive and ability of his soul, seeking the most intimate communion and fellowship with God. Man needs to worship God with the spiritual core of his life and being, trusting and resting in God's acceptance and love and care. **"Praise ye the LORD: for it is good to sing praises unto our God; for it is pleasant; and praise is comely" (Ps.147:1).** **"But thou art holy, O thou that inhabitest the praises of Israel" (Ps.22:3).** **"Let us be glad and rejoice, and give honour to him" (Re.19:7).** **"Praise ye the LORD. Sing unto the LORD a new song, and his praise in the congregation of saints" (Ps.149:1).** **"O magnify the LORD with me, and let us exalt his name together" (Ps.34:3).**

PROPHET	TIME/PLACE GIVEN	MAIN MESSAGE	PRACTICAL APPLICATION
HANANI **(Merciful)** **Known Facts** 1. Ministered to Judah, the Southern Kingdom (2 Chr.16:7). 2. Father of Jehu, the prophet (1 K.16:1-7). **Predictions and Messages** 1. The declaration that it was foolish for King Asa to rely on anyone other than the LORD (2 Chr.16:7-9). 2. The declaration that the LORD supports those who completely rely on Him (2 Chr. 16:9). **Scripture References** 2 Chr.16:7-10	**Time** *870 B.C., at the end of the reign of Asa, king of Judah, and just after King Asa made a treaty with the Arame-ans (Syrians).* **Place** *Jerusalem, in the palace of the king.*	We must rely totally on the LORD, and our dependence upon Him must not be passive. Rather, we must *actively seek* to trust the LORD more and more. For He searches the earth seeking people who are totally committed to Him. His eyes scan back and forth, looking for people who will place their lives fully into His hands. Furthermore, He longs to meet their needs and to strengthen and deliver them from all the hardships and temptations of life. But the people of Judah failed to actively trust and seek the Lord. Consequently, they were to suffer the judgment of God. **"And at that time Hanani the seer came to Asa king of Judah, and said unto him, Because thou hast relied on the king of Syria, and not relied on the LORD thy God, therefore is the host of the king of Syria escaped out of thine hand. Were not the Ethiopians and the Lubims a huge host, with very many chariots and horsemen? yet, because thou didst rely on the LORD, he delivered them into thine hand. For the eyes of the Lord run to and fro throughout the whole earth, to show himself strong in the behalf of them whose heart is perfect toward him. Herein thou hast done foolishly: therefore from henceforth thou shalt have wars" (2 Chr.16:7-9).**	Note the wonderful promise of Scripture: God works through the events of this world to meet the needs of His dear people, those who are fully committed to Him. No matter how terrible the trial or temptation, God moves within the event for one purpose and one purpose only: to deliver and to strengthen those who are fully committed to Him. A person who is fully committed can rest assured in this promise of the Lord. For the Lord will provide, protect and guide His dear people. Even in the moment of death, the Lord will transfer us into His presence—quicker than the eye can blink (2 Ti.4:18). **"Wait on the LORD: be of good courage, and he shall strengthen thine heart: wait, I say, on the LORD" (Ps.27:4).** **"And the Lord shall deliver me from every evil work, and will preserve me unto his heavenly kingdom: to whom be glory for ever and ever. Amen" (2 Ti.4:18).** **"Fear thou not; for I am with thee: be not dismayed; for I am thy God: I will strengthen thee; yea, I will help thee; yea, I will uphold thee with the right hand of my righteousness" (Is.41:10).** **"But the God of all grace, who hath called us unto his eternal glory by Christ Jesus, after that ye have suffered a while, make you perfect, stablish, strengthen, settle you" (1 Pe.5:10).**

PROPHET	TIME/PLACE GIVEN	MAIN MESSAGE	PRACTICAL APPLICATION
HEMAN **(Faithful)** **Known Facts** 1. Was the son of Joel (1 Chr.15:17). 2. Served as the seer to King David (1 Chr. 25:5). 3. Appointed by David to lead the congregational music (1 Chr. 25:1). 4. Born into the tribe of Levi (1 Chr.24:31). 5. Prophesied along with his family through the music (1 Chr. 25:1-8). **Predictions and Messages** None recorded. Since he is called a *seer,* he must have sung some of the LORD's predictions through the music of worship, as well as advised David about the results of certain royal decisions. **Scripture References** 1 Chr.25:1-8	**Time** *971 B.C., the last days of the life of King David. In these solemn times of final instructions from King David, Levites were assigned the task of making sure the worship of the LORD continued down through coming generations.* **Place** *Jerusalem, the Holy City.*	Heman praised the LORD with music and greatly encouraged the congregation of Israel in their worship of God. Leading music was his official position under King David. Heman prophesied while playing musical instruments. Just as Asaph, Heman's father, had faithfully served under King David, now Heman, Asaph's son, carried on the work. Heman carried on the legacy of his father, praising the LORD with music and spurring the people on in their devotion to the LORD. **"Moreover David and the captains of the host separated to the service of the sons of Asaph, and of Heman, and of Jeduthun, who should prophesy with harps, with psalteries, and with cymbals....Of Heman: the sons of Heman; Bukkiah, Mattaniah, Uzziel, Shebuel, and Jerimoth, Hananiah, Hanani, Eliathah, Giddalti, and Romamtiezer, Joshbekashah, Mallothi, Hothir, and Mahazioth: All these were the sons of Heman the king's seer in the words of God, to lift up the horn. And God gave to Heman fourteen sons and three daughters. All these were under the hands of their father for song in the house of the LORD, with cymbals, psalteries, and harps, for the service of the house of God, according to the king's order to Asaph, Jeduthun, and Heman" (1 Chr.25:1, 4-6).**	The importance of praise and worship cannot be overstressed. Because of all His good and perfect gifts—the LORD expects us to worship and praise His holy name. Music is one way, a very powerful way, to give praise to the Lord. We are to be talking about Christ, admonishing others in the Word of God and singing within our hearts the hymns of the church. We are to walk about rejoicing and praising the Lord within our hearts, being filled with the joy of the Lord and His Word, and bearing strong testimony for the Lord. **"Let the word of Christ dwell in you richly in all wisdom; teaching and admonishing one another in psalms and hymns and spiritual songs, singing with grace in your hearts to the Lord" (Col.3:16).**

PROPHET	TIME/PLACE GIVEN	MAIN MESSAGE	PRACTICAL APPLICATION
HOSEA (Salvation) **Known Facts** 1. Was the son of Beeri (Ho.1:1) 2. Prophesied for many years, his ministry extending through the reign of four kings (Ho.1:1). 3. Ministered to both the Northern and Southern Kingdoms (Ho.1:1). **Predictions and Messages** 1. The illustrated sermon about Hosea's unfaithful wife (Ho. 1:1–3:5). 2. The sermon about God's case against Israel, that they were full of sin and that they must repent (Ho.4:1–6:3). 3. The sermon about God's certain judgment of sin (Ho.6:4–10:15). 4. The sermon about God's love for Israel, even though they were rebellious (Ho. 11:1–13:16). 5. The prophecy that Christ would come out of Egypt (Ho. 11:1; Mt.2:15). 6. The sermon about God's call to repentance (Ho.14:1-3). 7. The promise of God's blessing coming upon the people (Ho.14:4-8). 8. The sermon about God's challenge to the wise listener (Ho.14:9). *Scripture References* The book of *Hosea*	**Time** *788–723 B.C., during the reigns of four Judean kings: Uzziah, Jotham, Ahaz, and Hezekiah. His ministry spawned the reigns of the last six kings of the Northern Kingdom, but he did not name these rulers. His ministry ended just before the fall of Samaria in 722 B.C.* **Place** *Both the Northern and Southern Kingdoms.*	Hosea had a hard life. He was given a very unusual command from God: to marry a prostitute. Hosea's life was an illustrated sermon of the unfaithfulness of the people, and how they had turned away from God. During the course of their marriage, Gomer, Hosea's wife, bore three children to Hosea, two of them fathered by someone else. Once, Hosea had to go to the public auction and buy his wife back from slavery. The shame of the situation was unbearable, which was the very message preached to the people. Israel should have been... • ashamed at the way they had been acting • ashamed at the way they had run away from the LORD • ashamed at the way they had gone after the lust of their flesh • ashamed at the way they had failed to serve God, in particular after all He had done for them Hosea preached bold, straightforward messages to the people, warning them that they must repent from their sin and seek the LORD. The people had been committing spiritual adultery against the LORD, running after the pleasures and the false gods of the world, pleasing their carnal nature. They needed to allow the LORD to break through the callousness of their hearts, for their souls were as unyielding as dry ground that had not been plowed. Otherwise, the hand of God's judgment would chastise them. But even in chastisement, God's people must remember that God disciplines His people. **"Come, and let us return unto the Lord: for he hath torn, and he will heal us; he hath smitten, and he will bind us up. After two days will he revive us: in the third day he will raise us up, and we shall live in his sight. Then shall we know, if we follow on to know the LORD: his going forth is prepared as the morning; and he shall come unto us as the rain, as the latter and former rain unto the earth" (Ho.6:1-3).**	God disciplines believers. He chastens, corrects, and rebukes believers. Now God does not cause bad and evil in life. God loves man. Therefore, God's concern is not to cause problems and pain for us; His concern is to deliver us through all the trouble and pain on earth and to save us for heaven and eternity. How does God do this? By chastising us. When we think of chastisement, we usually think of discipline and correction and it does mean this. But it also means to train and teach and instruct a person. Every true child of God knows the discipline of God's hand. His discipline differs with each of us, but each of us can recognize His discipline nevertheless. God stirs, guides, directs, teaches, trains, and instructs us all along the way, making us stronger and stronger in life and drawing us closer and closer to Him. **"I will be as the dew unto Israel: he shall grow as the lily, and cast forth his roots as Lebanon. His branches shall spread, and his beauty shall be as the olive tree, and his smell as Lebanon" (Ho.14:5-6).** **"That ye may be blameless and harmless, the sons of God without rebuke, in the midst of a crooked and perverse nation, among whom ye shine as lights in the world" (Ph.2:15).** **"Acquaint now thyself with him, and be at peace: thereby good shall come unto thee" (Jb.22:21).** **"I am crucified with Christ: nevertheless I live; yet not I, but Christ liveth in me: and the life which I now live in the flesh I live by the faith of the Son of God, who loved me, and gave himself for me" (Ga.2:20).**

(Cont. on next page)

PROPHET	TIME/PLACE GIVEN	MAIN MESSAGE	PRACTICAL APPLICATION
HOSEA (cont.)		"It is in my desire that I should chastise them; and the people shall be gathered against them, when they shall bind themselves in their two furrows. And Ephraim is as an heifer that is taught, and loveth to tread out the corn; but I passed over upon her fair neck: I will make Ephraim to ride; Judah shall plow, and Jacob shall break his clods. Sow to yourselves in righteousness, reap in mercy; break up your fallow ground: for it is time to seek the LORD, till he come and rain righteousness upon you. Ye have plowed wickedness, ye have reaped iniquity; ye have eaten the fruit of lies: because thou didst trust in thy way, in the multitude of thy mighty men" (Ho.10:10-13).	

PROPHET	TIME/PLACE GIVEN	MAIN MESSAGE	PRACTICAL APPLICATION
HULDAH (Life) **Known Facts** 1. Was the wife of Shallum, the keeper of the wardrobe (2 K. 22:14). 2. Lived in the Second Quarter of Jerusalem (2 K.22:14). **Predictions and Messages** 1. The prophecy that God would judge Jerusalem for idolatry, for ignoring God's Word (2 K.22:14-17; 2 Chr.34:22-25). 2. The prophecy that God would be kind to King Josiah, because Josiah had humbled himself, recognizing the sin of the people and the importance of heeding God's Word (2 K.22:18-20; 2 Chr. 34:26-28). **Scripture References** 2 K.22:14-20; 2 Chr. 34:22-28	**Time** *623 B.C., the eighteenth year of Josiah's reign, when King Josiah decided to repair the temple and a copy of the Law of Moses was found during the renovations.* **Place** *Jerusalem, the capital of Judah, the Southern Kingdom of Israel.*	King Josiah gave specific instructions to repair the temple of the LORD. While the repairs were being made, a copy of the Law was found in the temple. King Josiah read the Word of God and was aghast at what he read, because he realized that the people had grossly neglected the law and disobeyed the LORD's commandments. Earnestly wanting to understand what he had read, he commissioned a delegation of officials to seek a prophet who could explain God's Word to him. The delegation went to Huldah the prophetess who gave the following explanation: the penalties for disobeying the laws found written in the Book were to be executed, because the people had forsaken the LORD, worshipped false gods, and provoked the LORD to anger. God was going to judge and destroy the city of Jerusalem. But despite the terrifying message of judgment spoken by Huldah, the LORD had a very special message for King Josiah. Josiah had grieved over the people's sin, and he had humbled himself before the LORD in prayer and personal repentance. Because Josi-ah's heart was tender and responsive to the Word of God, Josiah would not personally experience the terrible judgment. It would come after Josiah's death. **"Thus saith the LORD God of Israel, Tell the man that sent you to me, Thus saith the LORD, Behold, I will bring evil upon this place, and upon the inhabitants thereof, even all the words of the book which the king of Judah hath read: Because they have forsaken me, and have burned incense unto other gods, that they might provoke me to anger with all the works of their hands; therefore my wrath shall be kindled against this place, and shall not be quenched. But...because thine heart was tender, and thou hast humbled thyself before the LORD, when thou heardest what I spake against this place, and against the inhabitants thereof, that they should become a desolation and a curse, and hast rent thy clothes, and wept before me; I also have heard thee, saith the LORD Behold therefore, I will gather thee unto thy fathers, and thou shalt be gathered into thy grave in peace; and thine eyes shall not see all the evil which I will bring upon this place" (2 K.22:15-20).**	What a lesson for us! To Josiah and his people, the Word of God had been lost. To many of us, the Word of God is neglected and ignored, even denied and rejected. Some of us act as though we do not believe the Bible is the written Word of God. After all, if we truly believed that the Bible is God's Word, we would read, study and feast upon it. The Bible truly is what it claims to be, God's Word; and if we ignore it and neglect it, what will God say to us when we face Him? Above all that is to be feared in this life is the neglect or denial of God and His Holy Word. Nothing on this earth is as important as doing exactly what God's Word says, obeying Him and keeping His commandments. But before we can keep His commandments, we must know what His commandments are. And there is only one way to learn God's commandments: study His Holy Word. **"Search the scriptures; for in them ye think ye have eternal life: and they are they which testify of me" (Jn.5:39).** **"These were more noble than those in Thessalonica, in that they received the word with all readiness of mind, and searched the scriptures daily, whether those things were so" (Ac.17:11).** **"Study to show thyself approved unto God, a workman that needeth not to be ashamed, rightly dividing the word of truth" (2 Ti.2:15).**

PROPHET	TIME/PLACE GIVEN	MAIN MESSAGE	PRACTICAL APPLICATION
IDDO **(Appointed)** **Known Facts** 1. Recorded some history about Solomon, Rehoboam, and Abijah (2 Chr.9:29). 2. Called a seer by the Scripture, a seer to whom God gave special vision against the wickedness and false worship of Jeroboam I (2 Chr.9:29). 3. Kept genealogical records (2 Chr.12:15). 4. Was not the "Iddo" who was the father of Zechariah the prophet. **Predictions and Messages** Wrote about the rebuke of Jeroboam given by the unnamed prophet at Bethel (1 K.13:1-5). **Scripture References** 2 Chr.9:29; 12:15; 13:22	**Time** *910 B.C., after the close of the ministry of Ahijah, the Shilonite, and after the reign of Jeroboam I, who put the idols of the golden calves at Dan and Bethel.* **Place** *Judah, the Southern Kingdom of Israel.*	Iddo was appointed by God to keep a record of Jeroboam's terrible wickedness and false worship and of the unknown prophets who rebuked the king. How did Iddo know about these events? The Scripture expressly states that Iddo was given special visions concerning Jeroboam (2 Chr.9:29). It should be noted that the unnamed prophet who gave the rebuke to Jeroboam did not remain faithful. He forgot God's Word and went off on his own, doing what he thought was right instead of following God's clear instructions. Apparently, because of the prophet's unfaithfulness, God later raised up Iddo to record the event so the world would have a permanent warning against the wickedness and the false worship of Jeroboam I. The unnamed prophet who cursed the altar at Bethel could not have been Iddo the seer because the unnamed prophet was killed before returning home (1 K.13:24). **"Now the rest of the acts of Solomon, first and last, are they not written in the book of Nathan the prophet, and in the prophecy of Ahijah the Shilonite, and in the visions of Iddo the seer against [about] Jeroboam the son of Nebat?" (2 Chr.9:29).** **"Now the acts of Rehoboam, first and last, are they not written in the book of Shemaiah the prophet, and of Iddo the seer concerning genealogies?" (2 Chr.12:15).** **"And the rest of the acts of Abijah, and his ways, and his sayings, are written in the story of the prophet Iddo" (2 Chr.13:22).**	Accountability is clearly taught in Scripture. The Lord is coming; and when He comes, He will judge the works of His servant and followers. All works of the believer will be inspected by the Lord so that each believer may be rewarded in perfect justice, receiving exactly what is due, whether good or bad (2 Co. 5:10). **"Therefore be ye also ready: for in such an hour as ye think not the Son of man cometh. Who then is a faithful and wise servant, whom his lord hath made ruler over his household, to give them meat in due season? Blessed is that servant whom his lord when he cometh shall find so doing" (Mt.24:44-46).** **"Moreover it is required in stewards, that a man be found faithful" (1 Co.4:2).** **"As every man hath received the gift, even so minister the same one to another, as good stewards of the manifold grace of God" (1 Pe.4:10).** **"Therefore, my beloved brethren, be ye stedfast, unmoveable, always abounding in the work of the Lord, forasmuch as ye know that your labour is not in vain in the Lord" (1 Co.15:58).** **"Take heed unto thyself, and unto the doctrine; continue in them: for in doing this thou shalt both save thyself, and them that hear thee" (1 Ti.4:16).**

PROPHET	TIME/PLACE GIVEN	MAIN MESSAGE	PRACTICAL APPLICATION
ISAIAH (Salvation is from the LORD) **Known Facts** 1. Was the son of Amoz (Is.1:1). 2. Ministered alongside Hosea the prophet. 3. Saw a tremendous vision of the LORD (Is.6). 4. Prophesied more about the Messiah than any other prophet. **Predictions and Messages** 1. A holy group of people will remain after the captivity (Is.6:11-13). 2. Christ, the Savior of the world, will live among men on the earth (Is.7:13-16). 3. Foreign armies will quickly invade and smash Samaria (Is. 8:1-4). 4. Christ will be the Wonderful Counselor (Is.9:1-7). 5. The Savior will come from the family of David (Is.11:1-6). 6. Judgment will come on wicked nations (Is.13:1–20:6). 7. The Servant of the LORD will come on a mission of mercy (Is.42:1-9). 8. A remnant of God's people will be gathered back to the promised land (Is. 43:1–45:25). 9. King Cyrus, who would help Israel many years later to return to the promised land, is called by name (Is. 45:1-13). 10. Yahweh is the only Savior (Is.45:18-25). 11. Babylon will fall (Is.47:1–48:15). 12. Christ will be the Suffering Servant and die an atoning death (Is.52:13–53:12). 13. An everlasting covenant will be given to Israel (Is.55:3-5). (cont. in col.3) **Scripture References** The book of *Isaiah*, 2 K.18–20	**Time** *740–690 B.C., during the reigns of Uzziah, Jotham, Ahaz, and Hezekiah.* **Place** *Jerusalem, the capital city of Judah.*	Isaiah's prophecies and sermons centered on the holiness of God and His desire to save mankind from his sin. Spurred on by his dramatic and unforgettable vision of God's holy throne, he warned people of coming disaster. But he also had many words of comfort to say from the LORD. Most importantly, Isaiah prophesied of the coming Savior, Who would bear the punishment for the sins of the world. But the main message of Isaiah is the same as the meaning of his name: "Salvation is from the LORD." It is essential to understand this biblical truth. For it is not just that salvation comes from the LORD (Jehovah/Yahweh) the One True God; but that salvation *only* comes from the LORD. It *only* comes through Jesus Christ, the Son of God, the Messiah whom the Father sent into the world to give His life as a ransom for the world. There is no other that can save. Only the LORD can rescue man from his desperately sinful situation. **"Behold, God is my salvation; I will trust, and not be afraid: for the LORD JEHOVAH is my strength and my song; he also is become my salvation" (Is.12:2).** **"And it shall be said in that day, Lo, this is our God; we have waited for him, and he will save us: this is the LORD; we have waited for him, we will be glad and rejoice in his salvation" (Is.25:9).** **"Tell ye, and bring them near; yea, let them take counsel together: who hath declared this from ancient time? who hath told it from that time? have not I the LORD? and there is no God else beside me; a just God and a Saviour; there is none beside me. Look unto me, and be ye saved, all the ends of the earth: for I am God, and there is none else" (Is.45:21-22).** **"But he was wounded for our transgressions, he was bruised for our iniquities: the chastisement of our peace was upon him; and with his stripes we are healed" (Is.53:5).** **Predictions and Messages** (cont. from col.1) 14. A Messiah will come to save (Is.61:1-11). 15. A description of the Millennium (Is.66:14-24).	The way to God is through Jesus Christ Himself. Jesus Christ alone saves, for there is no other exalted Lord. Therefore, no man can be saved by any other name other than the Lord's name. No teacher is capable enough, no prophet is noble enough, no minister is good enough to save himself, much less anyone else. Therefore, no matter the claim and no matter the strength of a person's name, no man has the name by which God can save people. All men are mortal. Therefore, no man can make another man immortal. But the Name which God uses to save men is eternal, the Name of the Lord Jesus Christ, the Son of God Himself. **"Jesus saith unto him, I am the way, the truth, and the life: no man cometh unto the Father, but by me." (Jn.14:6).** **"Neither is there salvation in any other: for there is none other name under heaven given among men, whereby we must be saved" (Ac.4:12).**

PROPHET	TIME/PLACE GIVEN	MAIN MESSAGE	PRACTICAL APPLICATION
JACOB/ISRAEL (Deceiver/Contender with God) **Known Facts** 1. Was the son of Isaac, son of Abraham (Ge. 25:19-26). 2. Fathered twelve sons, who became the heads of the twelve tribes of Israel (Ex.1:1-7). 3. Tricked his brother, Esau, into giving him the birthright; thus, the Messiah, the Savior of the world, came through Jacob's family (Ge.25:27-34). 4. Tricked his father, Isaac, into giving him the blessing of the firstborn, taking it from his brother, Esau (Ge.27:30-40). **Predictions and Messages** Jacob prophesied about the future of his twelve sons. The most important of all these prophetic utterances is that the Messiah, the Savior of the world, would come from the tribe of Judah. **Scripture References** Ge.48–49	**Time** *1858 B.C., after Jacob and his sons had sojourned in Egypt 17 years and more than 400 years before the Exodus.* **Place** *Goshen, a territory in the land of Egypt that was ruled by Pharaoh Sunusret III.*	In the later years of Jacob's life, he predicted the future of his twelve sons. His sons were to become the twelve tribes of Israel; consequently, Jacob was predicting the future of the nation of Israel and ultimately of the Savior to come, Jesus Christ. Although Jacob was not ordinarily a prophet, while on his deathbed, Jacob was anointed by God's Spirit to prophesy. The most important part of what Jacob predicted had to do with his son Judah. Judah would be the tribe from which the Messiah would arise. **"The sceptre shall not depart from Judah, nor a lawgiver from between his feet, until Shiloh come; and unto him shall the gathering of the people be" (Ge.49:10).**	Just think of this wonderful fact: God had a plan to save us before the world was ever made. How marvelous is God's love. And so that there would be no mistake, God revealed His plan in His Holy Word. God outlined very specific facts about Jesus Christ so that it would be clear that He is the Messiah, Son of God, and Savior of the world. Note just six of the essential facts, facts that clearly teach that Jesus Christ is the promised Seed, the Savior of the world: ➢ Jesus Christ is "the Lion of the tribe of Judah" (Re.5:5). ➢ Jesus Christ is the Prince of peace (Is.9:6). ➢ Jesus Christ gives rest to the human soul (Mt.11:29). ➢ Jesus Christ came to the earth so that we might have life, abundant life (Jn.10:10). ➢ Jesus Christ is the Savior and lord of the world and all owe their obedience to Him (Is.45:22-23; Ph.2:9-11). ➢ Jesus Christ came and gave His life on the cross for the redemption of humankind, and He will return again to gather His people unto Himself (Mk.13:27; Jn.14:1-3; 1 Th.4:16-18). **"And one of the elders saith unto me, Weep not: behold, the Lion of the tribe of Juda, the Root of David, hath prevailed to open the book, and to loose the seven seals thereof" (Re.5:5).** **"Wherefore God also hath highly exalted him, and given him a name which is above every name: That at the name of Jesus every knee should bow, of things in heaven, and things in earth, and things under the earth; And that every tongue should confess that Jesus Christ is Lord, to the glory of God the Father" (Ph.2:9-11).**

PROPHET	TIME/PLACE GIVEN	MAIN MESSAGE	PRACTICAL APPLICATION
JAHAZIEL (God sees me) **Known facts** 1. Was a Levite (2 Chr. 20:14). 2. Was the son of Zechariah (not the prophet) (2 Chr.20:14). 3. Descended from the lineage of Asaph (2 Chr. 20:14). 4. Served during the reign of Jehoshaphat (2 Chr.20:15). **Predictions and Messages** Prophesied that the LORD Himself would defeat the foreign coalition that was coming to attack (2 Chr. 20:15-17). **Scripture References** 2 Chr.20:14-18	**Time** *860 B.C., in the middle of the reign of Jehoshaphat and during the ministry of Elijah in the Northern Kingdom.* **Place** *Jerusalem, in the courtyard of the house of the LORD.*	During the reign of King Jehoshaphat, a coalition of three nations joined together to attack Judah. Instead of turning to foreign alliances as he had done in the past, Jehoshaphat prayed to God for help. As he waited for an answer, the Spirit of the LORD came upon Jahaziel, a Levite standing in the courtyard. Jahaziel prophesied that the LORD Himself would defeat the enemy (2 Chr.20:15-17). The next day when Judah went out to battle, they discovered the vast army of enemy soldiers lying dead all over the ground. During the night the LORD had apparently stirred the enemy soldiers to argue and fight among themselves. The result was catastrophic; and the enemy coalition, in a state of utter confusion, attacked and slaughtered each other. All Judah had to do was pick up the spoils. God had worked a wonderful miracle to rescue Judah and King Jehoshaphat (2 Chr.20:20-30). **"Then upon Jahaziel the son of Zechariah, the son of Benaiah, the son of Jeiel, the son of Mattaniah, a Levite of the sons of Asaph, came the Spirit of the Lord in the midst of the congregation; And he said, Hearken ye, all Judah, and ye inhabitants of Jerusalem, and thou king Jehoshaphat, Thus saith the Lord unto you, Be not afraid nor dismayed by reason of this great multitude; for the battle is not yours, but God's. To morrow go ye down against them: behold, they come up by the cliff of Ziz; and ye shall find them at the end of the brook, before the wilderness of Jeruel. Ye shall not need to fight in this battle: set yourselves, stand ye still, and see the salvation of the Lord with you, O Judah and Jerusalem: fear not, nor be dismayed; to morrow go out against them: for the Lord will be with you" (2 Chr.20:14-17).**	The lesson for us is a much needed one on the importance of prayer and fasting. Jehoshaphat and his people faced an overwhelming crisis, a crisis that they stood no chance of getting through—at least not successfully. Within their own strength, they would have been crushed. Therefore, they did the only thing they could do: they turned to the LORD. In order to show the LORD how sincere and desperate they were, they set aside a full day for fasting and prayer. They showed the LORD the depth of their sincerity, that they were willing to repent, to turn away from their sins and recommit their lives to Him anew. What a dynamic lesson for us! When we face a severe crisis, we too must seek to show the sincerity of our hearts and the depth of our need through fasting and prayer. We must commit ourselves to the LORD. Simply stated, seeking God through prayer and fasting is the way to secure the presence and power of the LORD. When we face a crisis or are longing for more of God's blessings, we should fast and pray often, showing the depth of our sincerity. **"Watch and pray, that ye enter not into temptation: the spirit indeed is willing, but the flesh is weak" (Mt.26:41).** **"But as for me, when they were sick, my clothing was sackcloth: I humbled my soul with fasting; and my prayer returned into mine own bosom" (Ps.35:13).**

PROPHET	TIME/PLACE GIVEN	MAIN MESSAGE	PRACTICAL APPLICATION
JEHU (Jehovah/Yahweh is He) **Known Facts** 1. Was the son of Hanani the seer (1 K.16:1). 2. Was not the king whom Elijah and Elisha anointed to be king of Israel and to execute the LORD's vengeance upon the household of Ahab. 3. Recorded history about some of the kings of Israel (2 Chr.20:34). **Predictions and Messages** 1. The family of King Baasha would be completely destroyed because of his terrible idolatry (1 K.16:1-3). 2. The wrath of the LORD would be upon Jehoshaphat because of the evil alliance he had made with King Ahab. However, because Jehoshaphat had removed the wicked idols of Ashtoreth, the LORD also saw the good in Jehoshaphat's heart (2 Chr.19:2-3). **Scripture References** 1 K.16:1-3, 12; 2 Chr. 19:1-3	**Time** *886 B.C., at the end of the reign of Baasha, king of Israel, to 853 B.C., during the reign of Jehoshaphat, king of Judah—the year Jehoshaphat made an alliance with the evil King Ahab of Israel.* **Place** *Samaria, the northern capital, in 886 B.C.; Jerusalem, the southern capital in 853 B.C.*	Before Israel conquered the land of Canaan, the LORD had strongly given them two warnings. First, they were to drive out the Canaanites completely and without mercy so that the evil of idolatry would not creep into the pure worship of the LORD. Second, they were not to intermarry with the heathen nations. 　The message of Jehu rekindled the fire of God's warning that had been given down through the centuries. But as before, His warnings through Jehu were not heeded. King Baasha followed after the false gods of idolatry. And King Jehoshaphat intermarried with the family of Ahab and Jezebel in order to form an alliance. God was angry because these kings, the leaders of His people, had rejected and disobeyed His Holy Word. They had ignored God's written message, so God raised up Jehu the prophet to once again warn the leaders and people: they must obey God's Word or face the judgment of God. **"Then the word of the LORD came to Jehu the son of Hanani against Baasha, saying, Forasmuch as I exalted thee out of the dust, and made thee prince over my people Israel; and thou hast walked in the way of Jeroboam, and hast made my people Israel to sin, to provoke me to anger with their sins; Behold, I will take away the posterity of Baasha, and the posterity of his house; and will make thy house like the house of Jeroboam the son of Nebat" (1 K.16:1-3).** **"And Jehu the son of Hanani the seer went out to meet him, and said to king Jehoshaphat, Shouldest thou help the ungodly, and love them that hate the LORD? therefore is wrath upon thee from before the LORD. Nevertheless there are good things found in thee, in that thou hast taken away the groves out of the land, and hast prepared thine heart to seek God" (2 Chr.19:2-3).**	God expects His followers to love everyone, even the wicked and those who hate God and His followers (Mt.5:44). But while loving and reaching out to the unbelievers of the world, the believer must never compromise his testimony for the LORD. He must never act against God's Word, disobeying the commandments of the LORD. He must always live a life of spiritual separation, a life that does not fellowship or form alliances with unbelievers. The believer must always take a stand for righteousness against wickedness. **"But now I have written unto you not to keep company, if any man that is called a brother be a fornicator, or covetous, or an idolater, or a railer, or a drunkard, or an extortioner; with such an one no not to eat" (1 Co.5:11).** **"If there come any unto you, and bring not this doctrine, receive him not into your house, neither bid him God speed: For he that biddeth him God speed is partaker of his evil deeds" (2 Jn.10-11).** **"Take heed to thyself, lest thou make a covenant with the inhabitants of the land whither thou goest, lest it be for a snare in the midst of thee" (Ex.34:12).** **"Blessed is the man that walketh not in the counsel of the ungodly, nor standeth in the way of sinners, nor sitteth in the seat of the scornful" (Ps.1:1).**

PROPHET	TIME/PLACE GIVEN	MAIN MESSAGE	PRACTICAL APPLICATION
JEREMIAH **(Yahweh will rise up)** **Known Facts** 1. Known as *the weeping prophet*. 2. Lived in Anathoth (Je.1:1; 29:27). 3. Was the son of Hilkiah (Je.1:1). 4. Served as a priest in the line of Abiathar. 5. Called as a youth. 6. Is thought to have written a large portion of the Bible: *1 & 2 Kings, Jeremiah, Lamentations*. **Predictions and Messages** 1. The vision of the almond branch (Je. 1:11-12). 2. The vision of the steaming pot (Je. 1:13-16). 3. The sermon about Israel's disobedience to God's Word and the coming judgment (Je. 2:1-6; 34:17; 35:17). 4. The sermon that Judah will be taken captive if they do not repent (Je.7:1-7; 26:1-7). 5. The prophecy that the house of the LORD will be made into a den of robbers (Je. 7:11; Mt.21:13). 6. The lesson of the linen waistband (Je. 13:1-10). 7. The prophecy of a great drought (Je.14:1-7). 8. The illustration of no comfort based upon the fact that Jeremiah remained unmarried (Je.16:1-6). 9. The sermon about observing the Sabbath (Je.17:20-27). 10. The illustration of the potter and the clay (Je.18:1-6). 11. The illustration of the broken jar (Je.19:1-6). 12. The sermon about administering righteous justice (Je.21:11-14). 13. The prophecy of the judgment against Jehoiachin (Je.22:29-30). (Cont. on next page)	**Time** *627–562 B.C., after the fall of Samaria until long after the final captivity of Judah, from King Josiah to King Gedaliah.* **Place** *Jerusalem until he was forced to go to Egypt.*	Many important prophecies and messages have been given to the world by the LORD through His prophet Jeremiah: Often the LORD aroused Jeremiah to use symbols or illustrated sermons to demonstrate the message of his prophecy. Of all his prophecies (some foretelling, but most preaching), one overall message comes through loud and clear: The LORD will rise up. Over and over Jeremiah's messages pointed out that God arises in favor of those who truly serve Him, and in judgment of those who refuse to hear His Word. God will arise and defend His faithful followers, delivering them from evil circumstances. God will even change His mind about judging a person if that person truly repents and then follows the LORD completely, trusting fully in His power to save. **"And the LORD hath sent unto you all his servants the prophets, rising early and sending them; but ye have not hearkened, nor inclined your ear to hear" (Je.25:4).** **"Behold, as the clay is in the potter's hand, so are ye in mine hand, O house of Israel. At what instant I shall speak concerning a nation, and concerning a kingdom, to pluck up, and to pull down, and to destroy it; If that nation, against whom I have pronounced, turn from their evil, I will repent of the evil that I thought to do unto them. And at what instant I shall speak concerning a nation, and concerning a kingdom, to build and to plant it; If it do evil in my sight, that it obey not my voice, then I will repent of the good, wherewith I said I would benefit them" (Je.18:6-10).** **"Therefore thus saith the LORD God of hosts, the God of Israel; Behold, I will bring upon Judah and upon all the inhabitants of Jerusalem all the evil that I have pronounced against them: because I have spoken unto them, but they have not heard; and I have called unto them, but they have not an-swered. And Jeremiah said unto the house of the Rechabites, Thus saith the LORD of hosts, the God of Israel; Because ye have obeyed the commandment of Jonadab your father, and kept all**	God is not some far away Being Who has no interest in what happens in the world. The LORD is the Creator of the earth and everything and everyone in it. He created every person for the purpose of worshipping Him, that men and women might have communion, a personal relationship, with Him. He is zealous for the souls of people. He rises up, calling for people to turn from sin and follow Him. But God will not rise up in our behalf forever. Eventually the time of judgment comes. And when the instant comes for judgment, judgment will fall swiftly and justly. Every person will be placed on the scales of judgment. It is then that a person must be on the side of Jesus Christ, God's Son. Always remember this unchanging fact: Without being on Christ's side, the scales of judgment will never tip in our favor, no matter what: ➤ No matter how much money we have given to the church or charity. ➤ No matter how many people we have helped. ➤ No matter how *good* we have been. ➤ No matter how much we have sacrificed. ➤ No matter how we die, even if we paid the supreme sacrifice of dying as a martyr. The teaching of Scripture is definite. It is crystal clear. Even if a person were to give his life for another, it would not remove his sin nor make him acceptable to God. Christ is the only way to become acceptable to God. **"For I have no pleasure in the death of him that dieth, saith the Lord GOD: wherefore turn yourselves, and live ye" (Eze.18:32).** **"Neither is there salvation in any other: for there is none other name under heaven given among men, whereby we must be saved" (Ac.4:12).**

PROPHET	TIME/PLACE GIVEN	MAIN MESSAGE	PRACTICAL APPLICATION
JEREMIAH (cont.) 14. The prophecy that the righteous Messiah would be from the family line of King David (Je.23:5-6; 33:15). 15. The vision of the good and the bad figs (Je.24:1-10). 16. The prophecy that Judah will be taken to Babylon as captives (Je.25:8-9). 17. The sermon about the cup of God's wrath (Je.25:15-17). 18. The illustration of the yoke—a symbol of the power of Nebucadnazzar, king of Babylon, over other nations (Je.27:1-6). 19. The prediction that Hananiah, the false prophet, will die (Je.27:1-6). 20. The prediction of the public execution of the false prophets, Ahab and Zedekiah, by the hand of Nebuchadnezzar, the invading Babylonian king (Je.29:21-23). 21. The prediction of the destruction of the family of Shemaiah (Je.29:30). 22. The prophecy of promised restoration to Israel (Je.30:1-3; 31:10). 23. The prophecy of the slaughter of the infants in Bethlehem at the time of Christ (Je.31:15; Mt.2:17). 24. A prophecy of the new eternal covenant to be made with Israel (Je.31:31-34; He. 8:8-12). 25. The prediction that King Zedekiah will die in captivity (Je. 34:4-5). 26. The prediction that Jehoiakim's family will all die (Je.36:30). **Scripture References** The book of *Jeremiah*; 2 Chr.35:25; 36:12, 21-22		his precepts, and done according unto all that he hath commanded you: Therefore thus saith the LORD of hosts, the God of Israel; Jonadab the son of Rechab shall not want a man to stand before me for ever" (Je.35:17-19).	

PROPHET	TIME/PLACE GIVEN	MAIN MESSAGE	PRACTICAL APPLICATION
JESUS CHRIST (Jehovah is Salvation) **Known Facts** 1. Is God's Son, the King of kings and LORD of lords, the Messiah, the Savior of the world (Mt.14:33; Mk.1:1; Lu. 1:35; 1 Ti.6:15; Re. 17:14; 19:16). 2. Is proclaimed by the Scriptures from Genesis to Revelation. 3. Stands forever as Prophet, Priest, and King (De.18:18; He. 5:6; Re.19:16). 4. Is the subject of endless facts too numerous to mention. **Predictions and Messages** 1. The proclamation that God wants to save every person ever born in the world (Jn.3:16). 2. The prophecy that the people would ask for Him to perform miracles of healing (Lu. 4:23). 3. The declaration that anyone who does not follow His teaching will be destroyed (Mt. 7:24-27). 4. The prophecy of the destruction of Jerusalem in A.D. 70 (Mt. 24:2; Mk.13:2). 5. The prophecy that the end of the world would come and terrible judgment would fall (Mt.24:1–25:46). 6. The prediction that Peter would deny the LORD three times in one night (Mt.26:34; Mk.14:30; Lu.22:34; Jn.13:38). 7. The prophecy that Christ would be killed and rise again on the third day (Mt.12:40; 17:22-23; 20:18-19; Mk.8:31; 9:31; 10:33-34; Lu.18:32-33). (cont. in col. 3) **Scripture References** De.18:15-18; Mt.21:11; Lu.24:19; Ac.7:37	**Time** *During the years of Roman Oppression* (A.D. 26-29) *the Pre-eminent Prophet, the Son of God Himself was sent into the world in human flesh to save and set free all people of all generations.* **Place** *The nation of Israel under Roman rule.*	No greater prophet than Christ has ever lived—or ever will live—for no one else is perfect; no other prophet is God in the flesh. No greater message has ever been proclaimed—or ever will be—than the great gospel message, the good news of salvation. The good news is that Jesus Christ has come so that we can escape death and hell and have eternal life through Christ's death upon the cross and His resurrection from the grave. Through Him we will live with God in perfection forever and ever. What more can be said? **"For God so loved the world, that he gave his only begotten Son, that whosoever believeth in him should not perish, but have everlasting life" (Jn.3:16).** **Predictions and Messages** (cont. from col. 1) 8. The prophecy that Christ would ascend to the right hand of the Father in heaven (Jn.6:62; 14:2-3; 16:10). 9. The prophecy that Christ would come again to judge the world, rewarding the faithful and punishing the wicked (Mt.10:42; 16:27; 22:13; 25:21; Re.22:12). 10. The prophecy that the end of this age and world was coming, coming suddenly and unexpectedly (Mt.24:1–25:46).	God loves every man, not just the religious and the good. He does not love only the people who love Him. He loves everyone, even the unlovely and the unloving, the unbelieving and the obstinate, the selfish and the greedy, the spiteful and the vengeful. God wants man to know His love. He wants to reach everyone in the world with His love. So God demonstrated His love in the most perfect way possible: He sent His Son into the world to reveal the truth of life to man and to pay the penalty of sin for man, in "behalf of man." Through the death of His Son upon the cross, God poured out the very life blood of His Son for man. No greater love could ever be expressed; no greater act could ever be carried out to show the depth of perfect love. **"Ho, every one that thirsteth, come ye to the waters, and he that hath no money; come ye, buy, and eat; yea, come, buy wine and milk without money and without price" (Is.55:1).** **"The Lord is not slack concerning his promise, as some men count slackness; but is longsuffering to us-ward, not willing that any should perish, but that all should come to repentance" (2 Pe.3:9).** **"But God commendeth his love toward us, in that, while we were yet sinners, Christ died for us" (Ro.5:8).** **"Who needeth not daily, as those high priests, to offer up sacrifice, first for his own sins, and then for the people's: for this he did once, when he offered up himself" (He.7:27).**

THE PROPHETS

PROPHET	TIME/PLACE GIVEN	MAIN MESSAGE	PRACTICAL APPLICATION
JOEL **(Yahweh is God)** **Known Facts** 1. Was the son of Pethuel (Joel 1:1). 2. Wrote the book of *Joel* (Joel 1:1). 3. Prophesied in Judah for a short time during the ministry of Elisha. **Predictions and Messages** 1. The prophecy of the coming devastating locust invasion (Joel 1:1–2:20). 2. The prophecy that restoration will come to Israel in abundance (Joel 2:21-27). 3. The prophecy of the Day of Pentecost (Joel 2:28-32; Ac.2:1-24). 4. The prophecy that a remnant will escape the coming judgment because they will call upon the LORD (Joel 2:32). 5. The prophecy of God's judgment against evil nations (Joel 3:1-19). 6. The prophecy of God's greatness and the truth that Jerusalem is protected by God (Joel 3:16-21). **Scripture References** The book of *Joel*; Ac.2:16	**Time** *830 B.C., during the ministry of Elisha and during the reign of Joash, king of Judah* **Place** *Jerusalem and Judah, the Southern Kingdom.*	Joel predicted several national disasters. In particular, Joel predicted that a locust invasion was going to wipe out the land, one that would be talked about for generations. The plague would be so terrible that no harvest would be left, none whatsoever. But Joel also prophesied that the Spirit of God would come in a special way and that there would be tremendous days of refreshing for those who stay true to the Lord. The message of Joel teaches that those who call upon the Lord will be saved. Judgment will come because of sin, but it will not last forever. Blessing and restoration will also be sent by God, but only for those who are called by God's name, only for those who truly acknowledge the Lord as the only true and living God. **"And it shall come to pass, *that* whosoever shall call on the name of the LORD shall be delivered: for in mount Zion and in Jerusalem shall be deliverance, as the LORD hath said, and in the remnant whom the LORD shall call" (Joel 2:32).**	Man is self-centered and rebellious toward God. He likes to feel independent. Consequently, man is dead to God and resistant to the pulling call and quickening power of God. Both God and man have a part in salvation. God calls. He attracts, draws, pulls, and tugs at the heart of man to come. But note: God will not call forever. When a man senses the call and pull of God, he must act then and there. He must believe and make the decision to follow Christ. **"I will take the cup of salvation, and call upon the name of the LORD" (Ps.116:13).** **"For whosoever shall call upon the name of the Lord shall be saved" (Ro.10:13).** **"This is the day which the LORD hath made; we will rejoice and be glad in it" (Ps.118:24).** **"For he saith, I have heard thee in a time accepted, and in the day of salvation have I succoured thee: behold, now is the accepted time; behold, now is the day of salvation" (2 Co.6:2).**

PROPHET	TIME/PLACE GIVEN	MAIN MESSAGE	PRACTICAL APPLICATION
JOHN THE APOSTLE (Jehovah/Yahweh has been gracious) **Known Facts** 1. Was the son of Zebedee, the brother of James (Mt.10:2). 2. Called away from the fishing trade to follow Christ (Mt.4:21). 3. Followed Christ closely. 4. Wrote the *Gospel of John*, the *Epistles of 1, 2, 3 John*, and the book of *Revelation*. 5. Was the only one of the twelve apostles not to be martyred, although an attempt was made against his life. **Predictions and Messages** The book of *Revelation* **Scripture References** The book of *John*, the *Epistles of 1, 2, 3 John*, and the book of *Revelation*	**Time** *A.D. 95, near the end of John's life.* **Place** *The island of Patmos, where John was exiled after a failed attempt to kill him by boiling him in oil.*	All prophecy points to this undeniable fact: Jesus Christ is the King of kings and LORD of lords. The book of *Revelation* shows Christ in all His glory and splendor. Christ is the Righteous Judge, the Righteous Lamb and the Righteous King. *Revelation* teaches us that to overcome the world, we must be fully committed to following Christ, the One Who has already overcome the world. God's purpose in revealing to John the great revelation of Christ is to focus attention upon the Lamb, the Lord Jesus Christ Himself, and His ultimate triumph over the world and its ungodliness and evil. God's purpose is to show the great redemption that He is preparing for all those who truly believe and follow His Son. God's purpose is to show man that he can be saved from the terrible things that are coming upon the earth. **"The Revelation of Jesus Christ, which God gave unto him, to show unto his servants things which must shortly come to pass; and he sent and signified it by his angel unto his servant John" (Re.1:1).** **"These things saith he that holdeth the seven stars in his right hand, who walketh in the midst of the seven golden candlesticks" (Re.2:1).** **"And every creature which is in heaven, and on the earth, and under the earth, and such as are in the sea, and all that are in them, heard I saying, Blessing, and honour, and glory, and power, be unto him that sitteth upon the throne, and unto the Lamb for ever and ever" (Re.5:13).** **"For the great day of his wrath is come; and who shall be able to stand?" (Re.6:17).** **"The testimony of Jesus is the spirit of prophecy" (Re.19:10).** **"And he hath on his vesture and on his thigh a name written, KING OF KINGS, AND LORD OF LORDS" (Re.19:16).**	God has appointed a day to judge the world. The day of judgment is set, already determined. God demands that all men repent now, repent of their sin and idolatry, from the vain imaginations of the world. Every man has a *concept*, a thought about God. But we should *seek* and find the only living and true God as revealed in the Holy Bible. This we do by reading and obeying His Word. Every person is personally responsible for forsaking the idols of this world and for finding God. Man is now to repent. God wants people to know that they can be saved while there is still time for them to repent. It is God's purpose to lead people to repentance and salvation, to lead them to the glorious inheritance of the great redemption that is to be given to all true followers of the Lord Jesus Christ. **"O Jerusalem, wash thine heart from wickedness, that thou mayest be saved. How long shall thy vain thoughts lodge within thee?" (Je.4:14).** **"And the times of this ignorance God winked at; but now commandeth all men every where to repent" (Ac.17:30).** **"But the heavens and the earth, which are now, by the same word are kept in store, reserved unto fire against the day of judgment and perdition of ungodly men" (2 Pe.3:7).** **"Knowing that of the Lord ye shall receive the reward of the inheritance: for ye serve the Lord Christ" (Col.3:24).**

PROPHET	TIME/PLACE GIVEN	MAIN MESSAGE	PRACTICAL APPLICATION
JOHN THE BAPTIST (Jehovah/Yahweh has been gracious) **Known Facts** 1. Was the son of Zacharias the priest and Elisabeth, and the first cousin of Jesus Christ (Lu.1:5-63). 2. Was the forerunner of Jesus Christ (Mal. 4:4-6; Mt.11:12-15; 17:10-13). 3. Lived and preached in the countryside and desert places of Palestine (Mt. 3:1-4). 3. Was jailed and beheaded by Herod (Mk.6:24-28). **Predictions and Messages** The unmistakable declaration that Jesus of Nazareth is the Christ, the sacrificial Lamb of God, Who would take away the sin of the world (Jn.1:29). **Scripture References** Mal.4:5; Mt.11:9; Mk.11:32; Lu.7:26; Jn.20:6	**Time** *A.D. 26, at the beginning of the earthly ministry of Jesus Christ.* **Place** *The Jordan River, about 20 miles east of Jerusalem.*	Jesus Christ is "the Lamb of God Who takes away the sin of the world" (Jn.1:29). Christ declared an astonishing thing: John the Baptist was the greatest man ever born of a woman. John was neither a prince nor a king. He was not a man of wealth, fame, or power. Who was he? Why would Christ make such a striking statement about him? He was simply a man who believed in the Messiah and who totally committed his life to that belief. But notice: John was chosen for this special task because he was so dedicated, so committed to God. John lived a life of total dedication to the Lord and of self-denial. He rejected the carnal, fleshly pleasures of this world and the coveting of its possessions. **"The next day John seeth Jesus coming unto him, and saith, Behold the Lamb of God, which taketh away the sin of the world" (Jn.1:29).**	God does not value a man by his social status nor by how far he gets in this world, but by his commitment to Jesus Christ. Christ declared John's eminence over all men; and in John, we have a blazing example of humility, of self-denial and commitment to God. And Christ declared that those who humble themselves will be greater still in the kingdom of God. It is an astonishing thought! But that is how much God values commitment and humility. **"Verily I say unto you, Among them that are born of women there hath not risen a greater than John the Baptist: notwithstanding he that is least in the kingdom of heaven is greater than he" (Mt.11:11).** **"For thus saith the high and lofty One that inhabiteth eternity, whose name is Holy; I dwell in the high and holy place, with him also that is of a contrite and humble spirit, to revive the spirit of the humble, and to revive the heart of the contrite ones" (Is.57:15).** **"And whosoever shall exalt himself shall be abased; and he that shall humble himself shall be exalted" (Mt.23:12).** **"Humble yourselves in the sight of the Lord, and he shall lift you up" (Js.4:10).**

PROPHET	TIME/PLACE GIVEN	MAIN MESSAGE	PRACTICAL APPLICATION
### JONAH (Dove) **Known Facts** 1. Was the son of Ammitai (2 K.14:25; Jona.1:1). 2. Wrote the book of *Jonah* (Jona.1:1). 3. Ministered to the Northern Kingdom of Israel (2 K.14:25). 4. Tried to resist obeying God's instructions to go to Nineveh (Jona.1:3). 5. Was called to a foreign nation (Jona.1:2). 6. Converted the entire city of Nineveh with his preaching (Jona. 3:5-10). 7. Lived in Gath-Hepher (2 K.14:25). 8. Quoted the Psalms repeatedly in his prayer for God to save him from the great fish (Jona.2:2-9) **Predictions and Messages** 1. Nineveh will be overthrown in forty days (Jona.3:4). 2. Israel's borders will be extended and restored to their original positions (2 K.14:25). **Scripture References** The book of *Jonah*; 2 K.14:25; Mt.12:39-41; 16:4	**Time** *780–765 B.C., during the reign of Jeroboam II, king of Israel.* **Place** *Nineveh, the capital of Assyria, about 500 miles east of Israel.*	Jonah was called by God to preach to Nineveh, the capital city of the Assyrians. But Jonah did not want to go. He had a simple reason: The Assyrians were known for their cruelty to his people. Their war strategy was not only designed to take control of lands, but to instill absolute terror in the people they were conquering. The Assyrians wanted to make sure that the people would be so afraid of them that they would not ever try to avoid paying the demanded tribute each year. So Jonah tried to run away from God. Jonah got on a ship sailing in the opposite direction. But God sent a storm. Jonah knew why the storm had come. At Jonah's request, the men of the ship threw him overboard. But God was gracious. He had a great fish prepared to swallow Jonah. When Jonah repented, the fish threw Jonah up onto the land. After recovering from his ordeal, the repentant prophet went to Nineveh and preached. The city repented too, and they were saved from judgment. The book of *Jonah* clearly teaches that no matter how evil a person is, God will forgive him if he truly repents. No place represented self-exaltation and opposition to God more than Nineveh. God was so angry with the Ninevites that their total destruction was only forty days away. Yet, when they repented, God relented, forgave Nineveh and spared the city. **"But I will sacrifice unto thee with the voice of thanksgiving; I will pay that that I have vowed. Salvation is of the LORD" (Jona.2:9).** **"But let man and beast be covered with sackcloth, and cry mightily unto God: yea, let them turn every one from his evil way, and from the violence that is in their hands. Who can tell if God will turn and repent, and turn away from his fierce anger, that we perish not? And God saw their works, that they turned from their evil way; and God repented of the evil, that he had said that he would do unto them; and he did it not" (Jona.3:8-10).**	We can now obtain the mercy of God. We need God to have mercy upon us because we have sinned against Him. We have done everything imaginable against God... • ignored Him • neglected Him • rebelled against Him • disobeyed Him • rejected Him • denied Him • cursed Him God will forgive our sins; He will have mercy upon us. But we must come to the throne of grace and ask for mercy. We must humble ourselves and fully acknowledge that mercy comes only through Christ Jesus. **"Who is a God like unto thee, that pardoneth iniquity, and passeth by the transgression of the remnant of her heritage? he retaineth not his anger for ever, because he delighteth in mercy" (Mi.7:18).**

PROPHET	TIME/PLACE GIVEN	MAIN MESSAGE	PRACTICAL APPLICATION
JOSEPH (He has added) **Known Facts** 1. Was the son of Jacob (Ge.29:22-24). 2. Was persecuted and sold into slavery by his brothers (Ge.37:4; 23-28). 3. Was forced to live in Egypt, a slave to Potiphar, falsely accused by his master's wife (Ec.39:1-2; 11-17). 4. Remained faithful to God (Ec.39:21-23). 5. Raised up after many years in prison to the throne of Egypt, second only to Pharaoh (Ge.41:39-41). 6. Had a gift from God for interpreting dreams (Ge.40:6-22). **Predictions and Messages** 1. Pharaoh's butler would be restored to his position (Ge.40:9-13). 2. Pharaoh's baker would be executed (Ge. 40:16-19). 3. Seven years of bountiful harvest would come to Egypt, but they would be followed by seven years of terrible famine (Ge.41:25-32). **Scripture References** Ge.40:1-23; 41:1-32	**Time** *1900–1885 B.C., during Joseph's reign as secondary only to Pharaoh of Egypt.* **Place** *Ancient Egypt, during the time of the Pharaohs.*	God is in complete control, and He carries out His plan regardless of the evil intentions of mankind. Joseph had all kinds of evil done against him. He was... • hated and persecuted by his brothers • sold into slavery • reported dead to his father • tempted by an immoral woman • falsely accused of adultery • imprisoned for twenty years Despite all of these awful experiences, God's purpose for Joseph was not stopped, not even hindered. At just the right time, God lifted Joseph up to be the second highest ranking official in Egypt, second only to Pharaoh himself. Even then Joseph did not take credit for himself. He gave all honor and praise to God for the interpretation of the dreams of Pharaoh. Through dreams, God delivered Joseph out of all his troubles and used him in a mighty way to save lives of multiplied thousands. **"Yet within three days shall Pharaoh lift up thine head, and restore thee unto thy place and thou shalt deliver Pharaoh's cup into his hand, after the former manner when thou wast his butler" (Ge.40:13).** **"Yet within three days shall Pharaoh lift up thy head from off thee, and shall hang thee on a tree; and the birds shall eat thy flesh from off thee" (Ge.40:19).** **"Behold, there come seven years of great plenty throughout all the land of Egypt: And there shall arise after them seven years of famine; and all the plenty shall be forgotten in the land of Egypt; and the famine shall consume the land" (Ge.41:29-30).** **"And for that the dream was doubled unto Pharaoh twice; it is because the thing is established by God, and God will shortly bring it to pass" (Ge.41:32).** **"But as for you, ye thought evil against me; but God meant it unto good, to bring to pass, as it is this day, to save much people alive" (Ge.50:20).**	God's plans overrule man's opposition. God's counsel controls the evil of men, subjecting and using even the wickedness of men to work all things out for good and to achieve His will for the earth. Not even rulers, no matter how powerful they are, can stop or hinder the hand of God. People do all kinds of evil, trying to control situations, trying to rule over someone or to exert some authority beyond their position. Just think for a moment of the terrible evil things people in the world do every day. They ... • hate • steal • murder • destroy • commit immorality • encourage others to sin • revile those who will not take part in their sin • persecute believers • even attempt to stamp out the gospel and the church But no matter what people do, they cannot stop the will of God and His plan. They will fail, for God has a plan and He will overrule and carry out His plan. Kings and rulers stand up and rally against God and His Christ, the Messiah. They stand against, stand in opposition to and in hostility toward Christ, foolishly thinking that they always have and always will overthrow God's plan. But they will fail. God's great plan of salvation will continue to march triumphantly down through the ages of history. Despite the railings of the devil and all his forces, God's church will go forward, will grow and conquer more and more. God rules and will continue to rule over all the evil plans of men. It is critical to know that God not only has a plan for the world, but for every person. The believer can rest assured that nothing can stop the plan God has for his life. **"The LORD bringeth the counsel of the heathen to nought: he maketh the devices of the people of none effect. The counsel of the LORD standeth for ever, the thoughts of his heart to all generations" (Ps.33:10-11).** **"Consider the work of God: for who can make that straight, which he hath made crooked?" (Ec.7:13).**

PROPHET	TIME/PLACE GIVEN	MAIN MESSAGE	PRACTICAL APPLICATION

MALACHI
(My messenger)
 	
Known Facts
1. Prophesied after the captivity in Judah.
2. Lived in the time of Nehemiah.
3. Was the last of the Old Testament writers.
 	
Predictions and Messages
1. The declaration that God has always loved Israel (Mal. 1:1-5).
2. The declaration that worship must be sincere (Mal.1:6-14).
3. The declaration that failing to honor the LORD results in a curse (Mal.2:1-9).
4. The declaration that marriage is holy before the LORD (Mal. 2:10-16).
5. The call to return to the LORD (Mal.2:17–3:7).
6. The declaration that a person must not rob God of His tithes and offering, not if the person wishes to be blessed by God. (Mal. 3:8-12).
7. The prophecy concerning the judgment of the wicked—they will not be spared (Mal.3:13-18).
8. The declaration that the righteous will triumph (Mal.4:1-3).
9. The prophecy that one like Elijah (John the Baptist) will come as a forerunner to the Messiah (Mal. 4:4-6; Mt. 11:12-15; 17:10-13).
 	
Scripture References
The book of *Malachi*
	Time
	430 B.C., about one hundred years after the Temple had been rebuilt under the direction of Haggai and Zechariah. Malachi was the last of the prophets to appear until Christ was born.
	
	Place
	Jerusalem, the capital city of the Southern Kingdom of Judah.
		Many of Malachi's listeners had participated in the great revivals of Ezra and Nehemiah and had fully committed their lives to the LORD. But now, just a few years later, they had slipped away from the LORD, turning back to a life of sin and neglecting the worship of the LORD and their duty to support the House of God (1:6-14; 3:6-12).
		The people were apathetic, complacent, only half-heartedly committed to the LORD. They needed to be called back to God. Thus God raised up Malachi to preach the utter necessity of repentance. In scathing sermon after scathing sermon, he pointed out the seriousness of Israel's sin. He called the people to return to the true worship of God.
		
		"For from the rising of the sun even unto the going down of the same my name shall be great among the Gentiles; and in every place incense shall be offered unto my name, and a pure offering: for my name shall be great among the heathen, saith the LORD of hosts" (Mal.1:11).
		"Even from the days of your fathers ye are gone away from mine ordinances, and have not kept them. Return unto me, and I will return unto you, saith the LORD of hosts" (Mal.3:7).
			True worship means more than ceremony, ritual and form. True worship must be sincere in heart, completely genuine.
			True worship, worship which truly draws us closer to the LORD must be five things:
			➢ Worshipping the only living and true God, the worship of Him and Him alone.
			➢ Approaching and seeking God's acceptance exactly as He says through the substitute sacrifice of the Lord Jesus Christ.
			➢ Living for God by following the Lord Jesus Christ and obeying His holy Word.
			➢ Hoping in the resurrection and not holding on to this world, but looking to the next.
			➢ Always seeking to have a pure conscience. This means...
			  • struggling, even to the point of pain, to keep a pure conscience
			  • struggling to be *void of offense*—to keep from stumbling and from causing others to stumble
			  • struggling to have a clear conscience toward both God and men
			
			"There shall no strange god be in thee; neither shalt thou worship any strange god" (Ps.81:9).
			"But the hour cometh, and now is, when the true worshippers shall worship the Father in spirit and in truth: for the Father seeketh such to worship him" (Jn.4:23).
			"That ye may approve things that are excellent; that ye may be sincere and without offence till the day of Christ" (Ph.1:10).

PROPHET	TIME/PLACE GIVEN	MAIN MESSAGE	PRACTICAL APPLICATION
MICAH **(Who Is Like Jehovah/Yahweh?)** **Known Facts** 1. Lived in Moresheth (Mi.1:1). 2. Wrote the book of *Micah* (Mi.1:1). 3. Ministered only a few years, but prophesied to both the Northern and Southern Kingdom (Mi.1:1). 4. Prophesied with Isaiah (Mi.1:1; Je.26:18; see Is.36-39). **Predictions and Messages** 1. The prophecy of God's judgment against Samaria and Jerusalem for idolatry (Mi.1). 2. The prophecy that judgment will come against social injustice (Mi.2:1-11). 3. The prophecy that there will be restoration for those remaining (Mi.2:12-13). 4. The prophecy that wicked leaders will be judged (Mi.3). 5. The prophecy of the promise of peace and purity of worship (Mi.4:1-5). 6. The prophecy that Israel will be made strong (Mi.4:6–5:1). 7. The prophecy that Christ will be born in Bethlehem (Mi.5:2-6; Mt.2:5-6). 8. The prophecy that Israel will be pure from the idolatry of the world (Mi.5:7-15). 9. A sermon about what God requires of a person (Mi.6). 10. A sermon concerning the terrible corruption among the people (Mi.7:1-6). 11. A prayer of repentance (Mi.7:7-11). 12. The prophecy about Israel's future restoration (Mi.7:12-20). **Scripture References** The book of *Micah*; Je.26:18; Mt. 2:5-6	**Time** *735–725 B.C., during the reigns of Jotham, Ahaz, and Hezekiah.* **Place** *Judea, Jerusalem, and Samaria.*	In Micah's day, the Assyrians were just a few years away (722 B.C.) from conquering Samaria, the capital of the Northern Kingdom of Israel. The Assyrians would be within easy striking distance of Jerusalem. Although Micah sternly warned Judah that a terrible situation was coming for the nation, the religious leaders would not believe it. Micah preached that not even God's holy mountain would be spared. But the leaders assumed that since the temple and God's Holy Place was in Jerusalem, the foreign invasion was impossible. Their pride would lead to their downfall. Micah warned the people: The LORD absolutely requires justice, mercy and humility. No matter how much we do in the name of the LORD, without these three things, we cannot hope to be acceptable before God. Without living the way God requires, judgment will come, terrible judgment. But if we walk humbly before people, showing mercy and executing justice, and truly worshipping the LORD, the LORD will accept us. For He accepts all who obey His Word and walk humbly before Him. **"Wherewith shall I come before the LORD, and bow myself before the high God? shall I come before him with burnt offerings, with calves of a year old? Will the LORD be pleased with thousands of rams, or with ten thousands of rivers of oil? shall I give my firstborn for my transgression, the fruit of my body for the sin of my soul? He hath showed thee, O man, what is good; and what doth the LORD require of thee, but to do justly, and to love mercy, and to walk humbly with thy God? The LORD's voice crieth unto the city, and the man of wisdom shall see thy name: hear ye the rod, and who hath appointed it" (Mi.6:6-9).**	God is to be feared, for He resists and stands opposed to the proud. The very thing we do not want to be is prideful. For the only way to escape the judgment of God's hand is to humble ourselves under His mighty hand. If we stand up to His hand, we will be stricken down; but if we humble ourselves under His hand, we will be protected and lifted up, exalted forever and ever. God is going to exalt the humble. The day is coming when the humble will be exalted in all the glory and majesty of Christ. They will be exalted to live with Christ, ruling and reigning with Him and serving Him throughout the entire universe. They will be with Christ, worshipping and serving Him forever and ever. **"Humble yourselves therefore under the mighty hand of God, that he may exalt you in due time" (1 Pe.5:6).** **"Humble yourselves in the sight of the Lord, and he shall lift you up" (Js.4:10).** **"But thou, O God, shalt bring them down into the pit of destruction: bloody and deceitful men shall not live out half their days; but I will trust in thee" (Ps.55:23).**

PROPHET	TIME/PLACE GIVEN	MAIN MESSAGE	PRACTICAL APPLICATION
MICAIAH **(Who is like Jehovah/Yahweh?)** **Known Facts** 1. Was the son of Imlah (1 K.22:8-9). 2. Suffered persecution for speaking the Word of the LORD (1 K. 22:24). **Predictions and Messages** 1. The prophecy that King Ahab of Israel and King Jehoshaphat of Judah would meet with disaster if they tried to battle the Aramean (Syrian) army (2 Chr.18:16). 2. The declaration that the LORD had allowed a lying spirit to influence the false prophets so that Ahab would be enticed into battle and to his doom (1 K.22:19-23; 2 Chr.18:18-22). **Scripture References** 1 K.22:1-37; 2 Chr.18:1-34	**Time** *853 B.C., at the end of the reign of King Ahab.* **Place** *Samaria, the capital of the Northern Kingdom.*	The battle at Ramoth-Gilead would be a disaster. Micaiah gave this prophetic message to King Ahab of Israel and King Jehoshaphat of Judah, who were planning to attack the Arameans (Syrians). Even though an attendant of the king warned Micaiah not to give a negative message to King Ahab, he advised that everyone go home and not fight the Arameans (Syrians) at this time. But the LORD had allowed a lying spirit to influence the false prophets to speak in unison so that Ahab would go against what the LORD had truly said. Because of his terribly wicked life and rule, God's longsuffering with Ahab had run its course. Now, it was time for Ahab to face the judgment of God. **"Then he said, I did see all Israel scattered upon the mountains, as sheep that have no shep-herd: and the LORD said, These have no master; let them return therefore every man to his house in peace" (2 Chr.18:16).** **"Now therefore, behold, the LORD hath put a lying spirit in the mouth of all these thy prophets, and the LORD hath spoken evil concerning thee" (1 K.22:23).**	We must guard ourselves against false prophets and false teachers, for the world is full of both. Far too often, the pulpits of the world are filled with false prophets who preach a doctrine other than the doctrine of Christ and His Holy Word. Their focus is not the Word of God but some other religious literature or some feel-good message. Ignoring the truth of God's Word, they seek the approval of their congregations by tickling their ears with messages of positive thinking and self-esteem or by placing too much emphasis on healing and miracles or a particular spiritual gift. These subjects are important, for they are each a part of God's Word. But the whole counsel of God's Word is to be proclaimed—both negative and positive. False prophets seek merely to captivate or pacify us, giving us messages they feel will secure our approval and enhance their own honor and recognition. We must guard against false teachers, wherever they come from, whatever position they have. False teachers mislead us into half-truths, lies and serious doctrinal error, which will lead to destruction. **"Beware of false prophets, which come to you in sheep's clothing, but inwardly they are ravening wolves" (Mt.7:15).**

PROPHET	TIME/PLACE GIVEN	MAIN MESSAGE	PRACTICAL APPLICATION
MOSES **(Drawn out)** **Known Facts** 1. Was the only prophet of Old Testament times with whom God spoke face-to-face (Ex.33:11). 2. Was born into the tribe of Levi (Ex. 6:16-20). 3. Was the son of Amram and Jochebed (Ex.6:20). 4. Was raised as an Egyptian (Ex.2:1-10; He.11:26-27). 5. Ran from Egypt to escape from a murder charge (Ex.2:11-15). 6. Heard God speak from the burning bush where God revealed His Name to him (Ex.3:1-14). 7. Led the people of Israel out of bondage (Ex.14:21-31). 8. Performed many miraculous signs (Ex. 4:30; 7:20; 8:6, 17; 9:10, 23; 10:13, 22; 14:21, 27). 9. Received the Law from God on Mt. Sinai (Ex.19:1–24:18). 10. Received the instructions for the Tabernacle from God on Mt. Sinai (Ex.25:1–31:18). 11. Was prevented from entering the promised land because he disobeyed God (De.34:4). 12. Wrote the Pentateuch, the first five books of the Bible. **Predictions and Messages** 1. The prophecy of the coming Messiah, the Savior of the world (De.18:15-18). 2. The Song of Moses: a prophecy concerning the future of Israel (De.32:1-43). 3. The Blessing of Moses: a prophecy concerning the future of each of the twelve tribes of Israel (De.33:1-29). (cont. on next page)	**Time** *1405 B.C., near the end of Moses' life.* **Place** *Across the Jordan from the promised land, in the Arabah, the dry desert land east of the Jordan River.*	Throughout his final forty years, Moses proclaimed the holiness and sovereignty of the LORD. During this time of leading the Israelites in the exodus from Egypt to the promised land of blessing, Moses wrote the first five books of the Bible (which is really one great book called *the Law* or *the Instruction* or *the Pentateuch*). In these Scriptures are found: 1. The beginnings of the world and the Israelite nation (*Genesis*). 2. The account of Israel's Exodus from Egypt, their escape from bondage: A type of escaping from the bondage of sin (*Exodus*). 3. The Law of God which Moses received on Mt. Sinai (*Exodus*). 4. The instructions for the Tabernacle, the place of worship: A picture of heaven (*Exodus*). 5. The instructions for the sacrifices, showing how man can approach God and be acceptable to God: The sacrifices foreshadowed Jesus Christ and His sacrifice as a sin offering. Through His sacrifice a person can be saved from sin, death and hell (*Leviticus*). 6. The journeys of the Israelite people: powerful lessons on following God (*Numbers*). 7. The sermons of Moses: the first studies concerning the nature and character of God and how people can follow and live for God (*Deuteronomy*). Thus the Mosaic Covenant, the law of God, lays the groundwork for all that follows in the Old Testament and in the Bible. For the Law points out that we need a Savior and that we must humbly come to God on His terms, offering the Sacrifice that He demands. The Law also points out that the believer must be separated from the world, refusing to live like the world and not being conformed to the world. The Law of Moses proclaims the very same message the entire Bible proclaims, that we need the salvation provided in Jesus Christ, God's Son. Moses preached his series of sermons (found in the book of *Deuteronomy*) as the children of Israel were getting ready to enter the promise Land. At the end of his life, he warned Israel not to forget the LORD, not to go astray as they had in the past.	The greatest commandment is clear: we must love God with all our heart, soul and strength. We must know that "the LORD our God *is* one LORD" (De.6:4). Note these three vital facts about this great declaration: ➢ God is the *only* living and true God, the only God Who can save, deliver and redeem. ➢ The Lord is our God. We have a personal relationship with the Lord. It is a daily experience. We are His people, the sheep of His pasture. Therefore, we should love, adore and worship Him. ➢ The Lord is one Lord. There is no other. The many false gods of the world exist only in the imaginations of people. Look at how great God is! No wonder the Scripture commands us to love God with our whole being, with all of our heart, soul, mind and strength. We are to love Him thoroughly, fully, completely—in every way for the rest of our lives. **"And he said unto them, Set your hearts unto all the words which I testify among you this day, which ye shall command your children to observe to do, all the words of this law. For it is not a vain thing for you; because it is your life: and through this thing ye shall prolong your days in the land, whither ye go over Jordan to possess it" (De.32:46-47).** **"For the law was given by Moses, but grace and truth came by Jesus Christ" (Jn.1:17).** **"Hear, O Israel: The LORD our God is one LORD: And thou shalt love the LORD thy God with all thine heart, and with all thy soul, and with all thy might" (De.6:4-5).**

PROPHET	TIME/PLACE GIVEN	MAIN MESSAGE	PRACTICAL APPLICATION
MOSES (cont.) **Scripture References** The books of *Genesis, Exodus, Leviticus, Numbers,* and *Deuteronomy;* Jos.8:31-32; 1 S.12:8; 1 K.8:56; 2 K.23:23-25; 1 Chr.22:13; Ps.90; Is.63:11-12; Mt.17:1-3		As he preached, Moses also broke out into song and prophesied of the future of Israel. Most importantly, Moses told of One Who would rise later, One Who would be similar to Moses. Moses spoke of the Messiah, Jesus Christ. Just as Moses spoke the words God gave him to speak so Jesus Christ spoke and did what the Father spoke and directed Him to do. Just as Moses delivered God's people from the bondage of Egypt so Christ delivers God's people from the bondage of sin. **"The LORD thy God will raise up unto thee a Prophet from the midst of thee, of thy brethren, like unto me; unto him ye shall hearken ... I will raise them up a Prophet from among their brethren, like unto thee, and will put my words in his mouth; and he shall speak unto them all that I shall command him"** (De.18:15, 18). **"Give ear, O ye heavens, and I will speak; and hear, O earth, the words of my mouth. My doctrine shall drop as the rain, my speech shall distil as the dew, as the small rain upon the tender herb, and as the showers upon the grass: Because I will publish the name of the LORD: ascribe ye greatness unto our God"** (De.32:1-3). **"And this is the blessing, wherewith Moses the man of God blessed the children of Israel before his death. And he said, The LORD came from Sinai, and rose up from Seir unto them; he shined forth from mount Paran, and he came with ten thousands of saints: from his right hand went a fiery law for them. Yea, he loved the people; all his saints are in thy hand: and they sat down at thy feet; every one shall receive of thy words"** (De.33:1-3).	

PROPHET	TIME/PLACE GIVEN	MAIN MESSAGE	PRACTICAL APPLICATION
NAHUM (Comfort) **Known Facts** 1. Lived in Elkosh (Na. 1:1). 2. Prophesied about Nineveh, just as Jonah did, but the Ninevites did not listen to Nahum, and they were destroyed (Na.2:8-13). 3. Wrote the book of *Nahum* (Na.1:1). **Predictions and Messages** 1. A poem about God's zeal for justice—His goodness and protection for those who take refuge in Him and His fierce wrath that falls upon the wicked (Na.1:2-8). 2. The doom of the Ninevites, who will be destroyed even though they have many weapons (Na.1:9-2:13). 3. A funeral poem about Nineveh, the greedy and violently wicked city (Na.3:1-19). **Scripture References** The book of *Nahum*; Is.52:7	**Time** *663–612 B.C., during the reign of Manasseh, Amon and Josiah.* **Place** *Judah, the Southern Kingdom and Nineveh, the capital city of Assyria, hundreds of miles from Jerusalem.*	The outcry of evil from Nineveh, the capital city of the Assyrians, reached up to God, calling out for judgment. And swift judgment was on the way. The Ninevites thought that they were unstoppable, too mighty to even be slowed down. For the small country of Judah, Nineveh personified the word terror. But Nahum had a message from God: the LORD is zealous, avenging His people and pouring out wrath upon His enemies. About one hundred years earlier, Nineveh had repented under conviction of Jonah's preaching to them. But now, the city had returned to its wicked and brutal ways, caring only about conquest and plunder, power and wealth. Nahum preached a message of total destruction. This time, the Ninevites did not repent and the judgment of God fell on the entire city. Tragically, the Ninevites had felt all powerful, so powerful that nothing or no one could harm their large fortified city. But when God pronounced judgment on them, nothing and no one could save them. Nineveh was destroyed in 663 B.C. **"God is jealous, and the LORD revengeth; the LORD revengeth, and is furious; the LORD will take vengeance on his adversaries, and he reserveth wrath for his enemies. The LORD is slow to anger, and great in power, and will not at all acquit the wicked: the LORD hath his way in the whirlwind and in the storm, and the clouds are the dust of his feet" (Na.1:2-3).** **"There is no healing of thy bruise; thy wound is grievous: all that hear the bruit [report] of thee shall clap the hands over thee: for upon whom hath not thy wickedness passed continually?" (Na.3:19).**	God is going to rectify all the injustices of the world. God's judgment is going to fall upon every person who has mistreated others. All unjust behavior of men will bear the terrible judgment of God, all the... • killing • stealing • mocking • fighting • cursing • prejudice • cheating • bitterness • abusing • hatred The list could go on and on, but the point is this: much of the world's behavior is evil and unjust. God *must judge* the world, for judgment is the righteous and just penalty for evil. All the injustices of the world must be corrected. God is going to judge the world. He is just and righteous Himself; therefore, His very nature demands that all the injustices and wrongs that men have inflicted upon others be judged and punished. God will execute justice and avenge His people. God sees the great need of His people, and God alone can meet their need. Therefore God, the just Judge of the universe, will avenge them of their adversaries (spiritual as well as human). Even now, when His people pray, continually bringing their case before God, He hears their plea, and He delivers them. And when the time comes, justice will be executed against the persecutors of His people. **"Shall not the Judge of all the earth do right?" (Ge.18:25).** **"And shall not God avenge his own elect, which cry day and night unto him, though he bear long with them? I tell you that he will avenge them speedily" (Lu.18:7-8).** **"So that a man shall say, Verily there is a reward for the righteous: verily he is a God that judgeth in the earth" (Ps.58:11).**

PROPHET	TIME/PLACE GIVEN	MAIN MESSAGE	PRACTICAL APPLICATION
NATHAN (He has given) **Known Facts** 1. Ministered during the time of the united kingdom under King David and King Solomon (2 S.7:1-5; 1 Chr. 17:1-4). 2. Named David's son Jedidiah (who later became known as Solomon) (2 S.12:25). 3. Stood with David against Adonijah the rebel, helping establish Solomon on the throne (1 K.1:8-46). 4. Wrote the history of the kingship of David and Solomon (1 Chr. 9:29; 2 Chr.29:25). **Predictions and Messages** 1. The prophecy that Israel would have a permanent dwelling place (2 S.7:4-10; 1 Chr.17:3-9). 2. The prophecy that God would establish David's family on the throne forever—that the Messiah, the King of kings, would come through David's family (2 S.7:11-17; 1 Chr.17:10-15). 3. The parable of the poor sheep owner—the exposure of David's sin of adultery (2 S.12:1-9; Ps.51:1). 4. The prophecy that David's household would be filled with death and violence (2 S.12:10). 5. The prophecy that David's secret sin of adultery would be punished by a public sin of adultery against him (2 S.12:11-12). (Cont. on next page)	**Time** *1003-931 B.C., during the reigns of King David and King Solomon when the kingdom of Israel was still united and strong.* **Place** *Jerusalem, the capital of Israel and the city chosen by God to place the temple.*	Through all the messages sent by God through Nathan the prophet, this one theme stands out: the LORD will greatly bless and defend all who honor Him. King David had a burning desire to build a temple for the LORD. Nathan had encouraged David to build the temple; but that very night God corrected Nathan, reversing his counsel to David. Nonetheless, God was very pleased with David and blessed David greatly because David honored Him with his whole heart. Note the tremendous blessings that Nathan predicted would be given to David by God: ➤ David would be given a position of astounding royalty and power. ➤ David would have the blessing of God's presence and guidance through the years. ➤ David would be given the power to conquer his enemies. ➤ David would be given an honorable name and reputation. ➤ David was assured that the promised land would be given to Israel. ➤ David was assured that he would receive future rest from all his enemies. ➤ David would receive a never ending dynasty. ➤ David would receive a Promise Seed raised up by God Himself. ➤ David would receive a kingdom established by God Himself. ➤ David was given the promise that the temple would be built by his son. ➤ David was given the promise of a descendant Who would be God's own Son. ➤ David was given the promise that the same descendant would be punished for sin. Although David did not build the temple, he honored God by his burning desire to build it. God greatly blessed David because he had a heart that longed to give honor to God.	God is good, and His goodness is overwhelming. But we live in a wicked world, a world where evil men roam and commit acts of terror, violence and lawlessness. In addition to evil men, the world is full of misfortune and hardship, temptation and trial. Yet in the midst of all the difficulties and problems of life, God's goodness shines through. For if we trust the Lord, He promises to save and deliver us and to meet our every need. No matter what the terrible circumstance, God will pour out His goodness upon us, strengthening and helping us to walk through any problem or difficulty. God is good, and He longs for us to trust Him. And if we trust Him, His goodness pours out the riches promises to us, promises that assure us of the most victorious and fruitful life imaginable. This is the wonderful promise of the incredible goodness of God. **"And he said unto him, Why callest thou me good? there is none good but one, that is, God: but if thou wilt enter into life, keep the commandments"** (Mt. 19:17). **"The LORD is my strength and my shield; my heart trusted in him, and I am helped: therefore my heart greatly rejoiceth; and with my song will I praise him"** (Ps.28:7). **"Thou art good, and doest good; teach me thy statutes"** (Ps.119:68). **"The LORD is good, a strong hold in the day of trouble; and he knoweth them that trust in him"** (Na.1:7).

PROPHET	TIME/PLACE GIVEN	MAIN MESSAGE	PRACTICAL APPLICATION
NATHAN (cont.) 6. The declaration that God had seen David's repentance and had forgiven him of his adultery (2 S.12:13). 7. The prophecy that David and Bathsheba son, born from their adulterous relationship, would die (2 S. 12:14). **Scripture References** 2 S.7:1-17; 1 K.1; 1 Chr.17		"And it came to pass that night, that the word of the LORD came unto Nathan, saying, Go and tell my servant David, Thus saith the LORD, Shalt thou build me an house for me to dwell in? Whereas I have not dwelt in any house since the time that I brought up the children of Israel out of Egypt, even to this day, but have walked in a tent and in a tabernacle. In all the places wherein I have walked with all the children of Israel spake I a word with any of the tribes of Israel, whom I commanded to feed my people Israel, saying, Why build ye not me an house of cedar? Now therefore so shalt thou say unto my servant David, Thus saith the LORD of hosts, I took thee from the sheepcote, from following the sheep, to be ruler over my people, over Israel: And I was with thee whithersoever thou wentest, and have cut off all thine enemies out of thy sight, and have made thee a great name, like unto the name of the great men that are in the earth. Moreover I will appoint a place for my people Israel, and will plant them, that they may dwell in a place of their own, and move no more; neither shall the children of wickedness afflict them any more, as beforetime, And as since the time that I commanded judges to be over my people Israel, and have caused thee to rest from all thine enemies. Also the LORD telleth thee that he will make thee an house. And when thy days be fulfilled, and thou shalt sleep with thy fathers, I will set up thy seed after thee, which shall proceed out of thy bowels, and I will establish his kingdom. He shall build an house for my name, and I will stablish the throne of his kingdom for ever. I will be his father, and he shall be my son. If he commit iniquity, I will chasten him with the rod of men, and with the stripes of the children of men: But my mercy shall not depart away from him, as I took it from Saul, whom I put away before thee. And thine house and thy kingdom shall be established for ever before thee: thy throne shall be established for ever" (2 S.7:4-17).	

PROPHET	TIME/PLACE GIVEN	MAIN MESSAGE	PRACTICAL APPLICATION
NOAH (Rest) **Known Facts** 1. Was the son of Lamech (Ge.5:28-29). 2. Found favor in the sight of God (Ge. 6:5-8). 3. Was a righteous man (Ge.6:9). 4. Received instruction from God to build an ark to preserve his family and some of each living animal (Ge.6:13-21). 5. Entered into a covenant with God to be saved (Ge.6:18). 6. Built the ark (Ge. 6:22). 7. Called a preacher of righteousness by the Scripture (2 Pe.2:5). 8. Was saved by following God's instructions (Ge.7:1-24). **Predictions and Messages** 1. Preached righteousness to a wicked generation (2 Pe.2:5). 2. Prophesied about the future of his three sons and their descendants (Ge.9:25-27). **Scripture References** Ge.5–8	**Time** *Unknown, but at least seven generations after Adam.* **Place** *The center of civilization, before the tower of Babel.*	Noah was a preacher of righteousness, warning people that the judgment of God was coming upon the whole world. What did he preach? Simply what God had told him—there is a consequence for sin. God would eventually withdraw his Spirit: His Spirit would not always strive with man, not forever. If man did not repent, the consequences of his sin would come upon him. Through the preaching of Noah, the Spirit of God was doing just what He does with people today when they hear the Word of God preached and taught in the power of God. He was convicting them of sin and of coming judgment. But the people were resisting and quenching the convictions of the Spirit. They were not listening to the voice of God struggling within their hearts. They wanted to live like they wanted, to do their own thing. Consequently, God had no choice. God had to give man a final warning: if man did not repent, God would withdraw His Spirit and let judgment fall upon the ungodliness and unrighteousness of men. **"And the LORD said, My spirit shall not always strive with man, for that he also is flesh: yet his days shall be an hundred and twenty years....And the LORD said, I will destroy man whom I have created from the face of the earth" (Ge.6:3, 7).** **"And he said, Cursed be Canaan; a servant of servants shall he be unto his brethren. And he said, Blessed be the LORD God of Shem; and Canaan shall be his servant. God shall enlarge Japheth, and he shall dwell in the tents of Shem; and Canaan shall be his servant" (Ge.9:25-27).** **"[God] spared not the old world, but saved Noah the eighth person, a preacher of righteousness, bringing in the flood upon the world of the ungodly" (2 Pe. 2:5).**	Judgment for sin is coming. Yet, people act as if the world will go on undisturbed. People act as if tomorrow will be just like today. The world continues in sin, foolishly rushing here and there, living as if there is no consequence for sin. Think how much our society is like the first society of earth. Think of the cult of beauty and sex, the power given to the immoral, the sin that runs wild all through society. But it will not continue forever. Just like Noah's day, eventually God will withdraw His Spirit and judgment will fall. The terrible wrath of God will be made known to the sinner, either when he dies, or when the judgment of God falls upon the entire world. A person simply cannot live an immoral and wicked life and hope that God will not notice. There are consequences for sin, serious consequences. **"But as the days of Noe were, so shall also the coming of the Son of man be. For as in the days that were before the flood they were eating and drinking, marrying and giving in marriage, until the day that Noe entered into the ark, and knew not until the flood came, and took them all away; so shall also the coming of the Son of man be" (Mt.24:37-39).** **"Now the works of the flesh are manifest, which are these; Adultery, fornication, uncleanness, lasciviousness, Idolatry, witchcraft, hatred, variance, emulations, wrath, strife, seditions, heresies, Envyings, murders, drunkenness, revellings, and such like: of the which I tell you before, as I have also told you in time past, that they which do such things shall not inherit the kingdom of God" (Ga.5:19-21).**

PROPHET	TIME/PLACE GIVEN	MAIN MESSAGE	PRACTICAL APPLICATION
OBADIAH (Servant of Jehovah/Yahweh) **Known Facts** 1. Wrote the book of *Obadiah* (Ob.1). 2. Ministered to Judah, the Southern Kingdom of Israel (Ob.16-17). **Predictions and Messages** 1. The prophecy of the doom of the nation of Edom (Ob.1-16). 2. The prophecy that Judah will overpower Edom, taking away Edom's territory and ending the evil nation's violence against Judah (Ob.17-21). **Scripture References** The book of *Obadiah*; 2 K.8:20-22; 2 Chr.21:8-20	**Time** *845 B.C., during the reign of King Jehoram of Judah.* **Place** *Judah, the Southern Kingdom of Israel.*	Edom will be overthrown because of her pride, a pride which led to a lifestyle of wickedness, and savage brutality, and violence against the Israelites down through the centuries. The Edomites were the descendants of Esau and were actually related to Judah. Because of their ancient relationship, the Edomites should have been good neighbors to Judah, but instead they were hostile, brutal and savage. Now, God would make them pay for their arrogance. Edom would suffer one invasion after the other over the next several centuries. Eventually, just as predicted, in the second century B.C., the Maccabees, who were Jewish zealots, finally conquered the Edomites and subjected them under the heel of Judah's authority. **"The vision of Obadiah. Thus saith the Lord GOD concerning Edom; We have heard a rumour from the LORD, and an ambassador is sent among the heathen, Arise ye, and let us rise up against her in battle" (Ob.1).** **"Though thou exalt thyself as the eagle, and though thou set thy nest among the stars, thence will I bring thee down, saith the LORD" (Ob.4).** **"But thou shouldest not have looked on the day of thy brother in the day that he became a stranger; neither shouldest thou have rejoiced over the children of Judah in the day of their destruction; neither shouldest thou have spoken proudly in the day of distress" (Ob.12).** **"For the day of the LORD is near upon all the heathen: as thou hast done, it shall be done unto thee: thy reward shall return upon thine own head" (Ob.15).**	All boasting and arrogance, pride and conceit is wrong. It is wrong to elevate ourselves above others, to think that we are *better* or *higher* than anyone else. God will severely judge all pride. **"Therefore pride compasseth them about as a chain; violence covereth them as a garment" (Ps.73:6).** **"And he shall spread forth his hands in the midst of them, as he that swimmeth spreadeth forth his hands to swim: and he shall bring down their pride together with the spoils of their hands" (Is.25:11).**

PROPHET	TIME/PLACE GIVEN	MAIN MESSAGE	PRACTICAL APPLICATION
PAUL (Small, little) **Known Facts** 1. Lived in Tarsus (Ac. 9:11; 21:39). 2. Was an apostle "born out of due time" (1 Co.15:8). 3. Was originally named *Saul* (Ac.13:9). 4. Persecuted the Christians, fiercely persecuted them (Ac.8:1–9:2). 5. Was converted in a dramatic confrontation with Christ (Ac. 9:3-9). 6. Became just as zealous for Christ as he had been for Judaism (2 Co.12:15). 7. Made many missionary journeys, taking the gospel to the world (Ac.13:1–28:31). 8. Was taken prisoner by the Roman empire (Ac.21:11-13; 25:14). 9. Wrote much of the New Testament. 10. Was martyred for the cause of Christ (by Nero in A.D. 64, according to church history). **Predictions and Messages** 1. A prophecy given to Paul by an angel—that all on board the ship caught in a storm would live (Ac.27:12-26). 2. A prophecy that Christ will return to the earth (Ph.3:20; 1 Th. 4:16. 3. A prophecy that the world will become very evil in the last times, with some saints even falling away (2 Th.2:3; 2 Ti. 3:1-7). 4. A prophecy that the saints of God will be resurrected (1 Co. 15:50-57; Ph.3:21; 1 Th.4:13-18). (cont. on next page)	**Time** *A.D. 35–64, all the years of Paul's life after his conversion.* **Place** *Various churches, homes and prisons, north and east of the Mediterranean Sea.*	If the message of Paul can be summed up in a few words, it can only be done in his own words: **"For I am not ashamed of the gospel of Christ: for it is the power of God unto salvation to every one that believeth; to the Jew first, and also to the Greek. For therein is the righteousness of God revealed from faith to faith: as it is written, The just shall live by faith" (Ro.1:16-17).** **"For though I preach the gospel, I have nothing to glory of: for necessity is laid upon me; yea, woe is unto me, if I preach not the gospel!" (1 Co.9:16).** What greater example could be set before us than the life of Paul, other than the life of Christ? The Apostle Paul was the apex of dedication and service, surpassed only by Christ Himself. Paul exhausted himself preaching and teaching the gospel, finally giving his life as a martyr. In all the preaching and prophecies of Paul, there was one clear point, one unmistakable focus: the gospel of Jesus Christ, the good news that Christ paid the price for sin on Calvary. Every person who accepts this, calling on the name of the Lord, can be saved from his sins. This person can become acceptable to God and be given a wonderful entrance into heaven, the place of eternal reward and receive the Spirit of God into his heart and life. With the presence of God's Spirit in his life, the believer has the power to live a conquering triumphant life through all the trials and temptations of life. No matter what the believer faces—even if it is the terrible evil of the last days—God empowers the believer to be "more than a conqueror" (Ro.8:37-39). Think, when the believer comes face-to-face with death, quicker than the eye can blink, the Lord transfers him to heaven, the place of eternal reward.	The hope of salvation—the forgiveness of sins, a victorious and conquering life and the gift of eternal life—all this has been entrusted into the hands of Paul and to all other believers. Note exactly what the Bible teaches: God's Word and the teaching of God's Word have been committed to men by the commandment of God. God's Word and the preaching of His Word are not an option. God commands that we take care of His Word, that we be good stewards of the truth of the gospel, that we preach and teach it to the whole world. **"Go ye therefore, and teach all nations, baptizing them in the name of the Father, and of the Son, and of the Holy Ghost: Teaching them to observe all things whatsoever I have commanded you: and, lo, I am with you alway, even unto the end of the world" (Mt.28:19-20).** **"And he said unto them, Go ye into all the world, and preach the gospel to every creature" (Mk. 16:15).** **"Then said Jesus to them again, Peace be unto you: as my Father hath sent me, even so send I you" (Jn.20:21).**

PROPHET	TIME/PLACE GIVEN	MAIN MESSAGE	PRACTICAL APPLICATION
PAUL (cont.) 5. A prophecy of the antichrist—that the man of sin will be revealed in the end time (2 Th.2:1-5). 6. A prophecy that Christ will receive those who are His into heaven and their eternal reward (1 Co.1:8). 7. A prophecy that death will be destroyed (1 Co.15:24-26). **Scripture References** Ac.8:1–28:31, the books of *Romans, 1 & 2 Corinthians, Galatians, Ephesians, Philippians, Colossians, 1 & 2 Thessalonians, 1 & 2 Timothy, Titus, Philemon*		"Nay, in all these things we are more than conquerors through him that loves us. For I am persuaded, that neither death, nor life, nor angels, nor principalities, nor powers, nor things present, nor things to come, Nor height, nor depth, nor any other creature, shall be able to separate us from the love of God, which is in Christ Jesus our Lord" (Ro.8:37-39). "And the Lord shall deliver me from every evil work, and will preserve *me* unto his heavenly kingdom: to whom *be* glory for ever and ever. Amen" (2 Ti.4:18).	

PROPHET	TIME/PLACE GIVEN	MAIN MESSAGE	PRACTICAL APPLICATION
SAMUEL **(God hears)** **Known Facts** 1. Dedicated to God from birth (1 S.1:11; 2:18). 2. Was favored highly with God and man (1 S.2:26). 3. Was given prophecies from God even as a boy (1 S.3:1-18). 4. Was recognized as a prophet to all Israel (1 S.3:20). 5. Lived in Ramah (1 S. 7:17). 6. Appointed his sons as judges, but they were wicked (1 S.8:3). 7. Anointed Saul as king (1 S.10:1). 8. Recorded events of David's reign and the regulations to govern the king and control his power (1 S.10:25; 1 Chr.29:29). 9. Faithfully served as a judge all his days (1 S.12:1-5). 10. Called down rain and thunder during the dry season—a sign that Samuel was God's spokesman (1 S. 12:16-18). 11. Anointed David as king over Israel (1 S. 16:1, 13). **Predictions and Messages** 1. The prophecy that judgment would fall on the family of Eli, the priest, because of his evil sons (1 S. 3:11-14; 4:17-22). 2. The prophecy that if Israel would get rid of their false gods, the LORD would help Israel defeat the Philistines (1 S.7:3). 3. The prophecy that when Israel cried out to the LORD because of the severe rule of the king they had insisted on, the LORD would not hear them (1 S.8:10-18). (cont. on next page)	**Time** *1095-1015 B.C., about forty years before King Saul and during most of his reign.* **Place** *In the center regions of Israel, serving as judge to the entire nation. In order to hear all the cases and judge Israel rightly, Samuel traveled on a regular yearly circuit all his life from Bethel to Gilgal to Mizpeh and back to his home in Ramah (1 S. 7:15-17).*	The messages, ministry and life of Samuel the prophet can be summed up in three words: "Serve the LORD." With this simple message, Samuel guided and judged the people of Israel for eighty years. Samuel encouraged the people: 1. To serve the LORD with all their heart (1 S.12:20, 24). 2. To serve the LORD and not to turn aside (1 S.12:20). 3. To serve the LORD in truth (1 S.12:24). 4. To serve the LORD, considering what great things He had done for them (1 S.12:24). Samuel's testimony is one of the strongest records of faithfulness ever lived. In Samuel's lifetime, he witnessed some of the most horrifying evil and wickedness ever committed upon the face of the earth, even by the leadership of Israel. For example, Eli, the priest who reared and trained him, would not control his own wicked sons. They committed the most vile acts of immorality imaginable—at the very tabernacle itself, the worship center of Israel (1 S.2;22). Saul, whom God had raised up to serve as king, turned out to be a great disappointment. Despite Samuel's great trust in him, Saul disobeyed God time and time again, until God finally had to remove him from the kingship and instruct Samuel to anoint another (David). But Samuel was faithful, faithful to the end. Through all the years he stayed true to the LORD despite all the horrifying evil of society.	Just imagine the impact Samuel's life and ministry had. There was no one, not a single person who could accuse Samuel of wrongdoing. He had lived a righteous life and served faithfully throughout all the years, throughout all the days of his life. What a testimony! What a dynamic, living example for us. We must live righteous lives, keeping all the commandments of God, obeying Him in all that He says. We must be faithful and diligent in all that we do. This is the strong declaration of God's Holy Word: **"Moreover it is required in stewards, that a man be found faithful" (1 Co.4:2).** **"Therefore, my beloved brethren, be ye stedfast, unmoveable, always abounding in the work of the Lord, forasmuch as ye know that your labour is not in vain in the Lord" (1 Co.15:58).** **"As every man hath received the gift, even so minister the same one to another, as good stewards of the manifold grace of God" (1 Pe.4:10).** **"These shall make war with the Lamb, and the Lamb shall overcome them: for he is Lord of lords, and King of kings: and they that are with him are called, and chosen, and faithful" (Re.17:14).** **"Let your heart therefore be perfect with the LORD our God, to walk in his statutes, and to keep his commandments, as at this day" (1 K.8:61).**

PROPHET	TIME/PLACE GIVEN	MAIN MESSAGE	PRACTICAL APPLICATION
SAMUEL (cont.) 4. The declaration that Saul's donkeys had been found (1 S.9:20). 5. The prophecy that God would change Saul into a different man so that he could serve as king (1 S.10:6). 6. The sermon of the history of Israel—a strong message that God would be with Israel so long as they faithfully obeyed Him (1 S.12:6-15). 7. The prophecy that the LORD would take Israel out of the promised land if they did evil (1 S.12:24-25). 8. The declaration that God had rejected Saul and chosen another (David) to be king (1 S.13:13-14; 15:17-29; 28:16-17). 9. The message from God to Samuel, that God was sorry he had made Saul king, because Saul had been so disobedient (1 S.15:10-11). 10. The prophecy that Saul and Jonathan would die the next day in battle (1 S. 28:18-19). **Scripture References** 1 S.1:1-25:1; 28:8-20; Je.15:1		"If ye will fear the LORD, and serve him, and obey his voice, and not rebel against the commandment of the LORD, then shall both ye and also the king that reigneth over you continue following the LORD your God: But if ye will not obey the voice of the LORD, but rebel against the commandment of the LORD, then shall the hand of the LORD be against you, as it was against your fathers....And Samuel said unto the people, Fear not: ye have done all this wickedness: yet turn not aside from following the LORD, but serve the LORD with all your heart; And turn ye not aside: for then should ye go after vain things, which cannot profit nor deliver; for they are vain. For the LORD will not forsake his people for his great name's sake: because it hath pleased the LORD to make you his people. Moreover as for me, God forbid that I should sin against the LORD in ceasing to pray for you: but I will teach you the good and the right way: Only fear the LORD, and serve him in truth with all your heart: for consider how great things he hath done for you. But if ye shall still do wickedly, ye shall be consumed, both ye and your king" (1 S.12:14-15, 20-25). "And Samuel said, Hath the LORD as great delight in burnt offerings and sacrifices, as in obeying the voice of the LORD? Behold, to obey is better than sacrifice, and to hearken than the fat of rams. For rebellion is as the sin of witchcraft, and stubbornness is as iniquity and idolatry" (1 S.15:22-23).	

PROPHET	TIME/PLACE GIVEN	MAIN MESSAGE	PRACTICAL APPLICATION
SHEMAIAH (Jehovah/Yahweh hears) **Known Facts** 1. Recorded the history of Rehoboam (2 Chr. 11:15). 2. Ministered to Judah, the Southern Kingdom (1 K.12:22; 2 Chr.12:5). **Predictions and Messages** 1. The message to King Rehoboam that the rebellion of Jeroboam and the northern tribes of Israel was the will of God and that Rehoboam should not try to stop the uprising (1 K.12:22-24; 2 Chr.11:2-4). 2. The prophecy that Jerusalem would be given into the hand of Egypt's King Shishak because the people had been unfaithful, forsaking the Law of the LORD (2 Chr.12:5). 3. The prophecy that the people would become servants of Shishak, but Jerusalem would not be destroyed, because the people had repented at the LORD's first message (see #2; 2 Chr.12:7-8). **Scripture References** 1 K.12:22-24; 2 Chr.11:2-4; 12:5-8, 15 (cont. on next page)	**Time** *926 B.C., the fifth year of the reign of Rehoboam, king of Judah.* **Place** *Jerusalem, the capital of Judah, the Southern Kingdom of Israel.*	Shortly after the ten northern tribes had revolted and formed the Northern Kingdom, Rehoboam mobilized an army of 180,000 soldiers to put down the rebellion. His purpose was to invade the northern tribes and permanently subject them under his rule. But while marching north to attack, God's prophet Shemaiah confronted Rehoboam. God's prophet had a stark warning for the king and the leaders of Judah (vv.2-4). They were not to fight against their brothers, the Israelites. Rather they were to return home, for the ruptured, divided kingdom was of God, the work of His hands. Hearing this stern warning from the prophet, the king and the people obeyed the LORD and returned home. But five years later when the scene refocuses upon Rehoboam and Judah, tragic differences are seen in the life of the king and people. They have turned away from the LORD, disobeying His Word and committing apostasy against Him. The hearts of Rehoboam and the people have wandered away from the LORD. As a result Shemaiah, the prophet, had another message for the king and people: Shishak, the Egyptian king was going to destroy Jerusalem. Upon hearing this message, the leaders quickly humbled themselves before the LORD. Thus God sent Shemaiah back with an amended message: Shishak would still attack and some of the people would be taken away as slaves, but the city of Jerusalem would remain. Note: the more severe judgment of God was averted because the people repented, but they still suffered the consequences for their sin. **"But the word of God came unto Shemaiah the man of God, saying, Speak unto Rehoboam, the son of Solomon, king of Judah, and unto all the house of Judah and Benjamin, and to the remnant of the people, saying, Thus saith the LORD, Ye shall not go up, nor fight against your brethren the children of Israel: return every man to his house; for this thing is from me. They hearkened therefore to the word of the LORD, and returned to depart, according to the word of the Lord" (1 K.12:22-24).**	God demands obedience, a lifetime of obedience. We are to always obey God's Holy Word, His commandments. Obeying God today and disobeying Him tomorrow does not make us acceptable to God. A life of inconsistency—obeying this week and disobeying next week—exposes a heart of insincerity and hypocrisy, a heart of dishonesty before God. A true profession of Christ means that we keep God's Word, obey His holy commandments. When we keep some commandments now and break other commandments later and continue a path of inconsistency, this is a life of deception and duplicity. Professing to be a follower of the LORD and consistently breaking His commandments is living a double life. It is attempting to establish a relationship with the LORD that is phony, double-dealing, shifty—a fake life that professes to obey God by living an unfaithful, untruthful life—a hypocritical life. **"Not every one that saith unto me, Lord, Lord, shall enter into the kingdom of heaven; but he that doeth the will of my Father which is in heaven. Many will say to me in that day, Lord, Lord, have we not prophesied in thy name? and in thy name have cast out devils? and in thy name done many wonderful works? And then will I profess unto them, I never knew you: depart from me, ye that work iniquity" (Mt.7:21-23).** **"Ye are my friends, if ye do whatsoever I command you" (Jn.15:14).** **"O that there were such an heart in them, that they would fear me, and keep all my commandments always, that it might be well with them, and with their children for ever!" (De.5:29).** **"Draw nigh to God, and he will draw nigh to you. Cleanse your hands, ye sinners; and purify your hearts, ye double minded" (Js.4:8).**

PROPHET	TIME/PLACE GIVEN	MAIN MESSAGE	PRACTICAL APPLICATION
SHEMAIAH (cont.)		"Then came Shemaiah the prophet to Rehoboam, and to the princes of Judah, that were gathered together to Jerusalem because of Shishak, and said unto them, Thus saith the LORD, Ye have forsaken me, and therefore have I also left you in the hand of Shishak. Whereupon the princes of Israel and the king humbled themselves; and they said, The LORD is righteous. And when the LORD saw that they humbled themselves, the word of the LORD came to Shemaiah, saying, They have humbled themselves; therefore I will not destroy them, but I will grant them some deliverance; and my wrath shall not be poured out upon Jerusalem by the hand of Shishak. Nevertheless they shall be his servants; that they may know my service, and the service of the kingdoms of the countries" (2 Chr.12:5-8).	

PROPHET	TIME/PLACE GIVEN	MAIN MESSAGE	PRACTICAL APPLICATION
The UNNAMED PROPHET who prophesied total victory for King Ahab of Israel over the Arameans (Syrians) **Known Facts** Delivered a message from God to King Ahab (1 K. 20:28). **Predictions and Messages** The entire Aramean (Syrian) army would be given into the hand of King Ahab. **Scripture References** 1 K.20:26-30	**Time** *855 B.C., during the reign of Ahab of Israel and during the ministry of Elijah the prophet.* **Place** *Samaria, the capital of the Northern Kingdom of Israel.*	The LORD sent His prophet to King Ahab once more to announce that He would deliver the vast army of the Arameans (Syrians) into the hands of the Israelites. Through the victory Ahab was to learn a great truth: The LORD is sovereign; His power is not partial or limited, but absolute. The LORD was going to prove that He was not just one god among many, not just a god of the hills as the Syrians falsely believed. He alone is the LORD (Jehovah/Yahweh), the only true and living God. **"And there came a man of God, and spake unto the king of Israel, and said, Thus saith the LORD, Because the Syrians have said, The LORD is God of the hills, but he is not God of the valleys, therefore will I deliver all this great multitude into thine hand, and ye shall know that I am the LORD" (1 K.20:28).**	The lesson for us is a much needed one: The LORD's sovereignty (His power) is not limited or partial, but absolute. The LORD is sovereign everywhere, throughout the entire universe. He is sovereign over all nations and kingdoms upon earth and in heaven. No limitation whatsoever hampers God's sovereignty or power. God controls all events and all happenings. And His sovereign power will eventually end all evil. **"For he must reign, till he hath put all enemies under his feet" (1 Co.15:25).** **"The LORD shall reign for ever and ever" (Ex.15:18).** **"The LORD hath prepared his throne in the heavens; and his kingdom ruleth over all" (Ps. 103:19).**

PROPHET	TIME/PLACE GIVEN	MAIN MESSAGE	PRACTICAL APPLICATION
The UNNAMED PROPHET who prophesied a victory for King Ahab of Israel over the Arameans (Syrians) **Known Facts** Delivered two messages from God to King Ahab (1 K.20:13, 22). **Predictions and Messages** 1. The prophecy that the LORD would deliver the Arameans (Syrians) into the hand of King Ahab (1 K. 20:13-15). 2. The prophecy that the Arameans would attack again the next year (1 K.20:22). **Scripture References** 1 K.20:1-25	**Time** *856 B.C., during the reign of Ahab of Israel and during the ministry of Elijah the prophet.* **Place** *Samaria, the capital of the Northern Kingdom of Israel.*	The LORD sent His prophet to King Ahab with a very special message during a very difficult time. The massive Syrian army was surrounding Ahab's capital city of Samaria. The situation seemed utterly hopeless. But the LORD longed to reach the heart of Ahab, longed for Ahab to stop Jezebel's savage purge of God's prophets and the worship of the LORD. Thus the LORD sent an unnamed prophet to Ahab, announcing that God was going to give a miraculous victory to the king for one specific purpose: to prove that He alone is God, the only true and living God. Ahab followed the battle instructions given him and achieved a great victory. Later, after the battle, the prophet came again and warned Ahab that the Arameans would attack again the next year. Now note this fact: even this warning should have aroused Ahab to repent, for God was still reaching out to him in compassion, patiently longing for him to turn from his wickedness, to acknowledge the one and only true God. But Ahab's heart was stubborn and unyielding. **"Thus saith the LORD, Hast thou seen all this great multitude? behold, I will deliver it into thine hand this day; and thou shalt know that I am the LORD. And Ahab said, By whom? And he said, Thus saith the LORD, Even by the young men of the princes of the provinces. Then he said, Who shall order the battle? And he answered, Thou. Then he numbered the young men of the princes of the provinces, and they were two hundred and thirty two: and after them he numbered all the people, even all the children of Israel, being seven thousand" (1 K.20:13-15).** **"Go, strengthen thyself, and mark, and see what thou doest: for at the return of the year the king of Syria will come up against thee" (1 K.20:22).**	God's purpose for helping us in times of trouble is to prove that He alone is God. There is only one true and living God, only one Creator, only one Sovereign LORD and Majesty of the universe. All other gods are false, deceivers that mislead and entrap human beings and capture their loyalty. And the terrible tragedy is this: if we are deceived into following and worshipping false gods, we condemn and doom ourselves. When hardships and misfortunes fall upon us, there is no living God to help us; for we are following false gods that are lifeless and powerless to help. We must recognize the LORD, the only true God. We must trust in the only One Who can help us in time of trouble. **"Thou, even thou, art LORD alone; thou hast made heaven, the heaven of heavens, with all their host, the earth, and all things that are therein, the seas, and all that is therein, and thou preservest them all; and the host of heaven worshippeth thee" (Neh.9:6).** **"Of old hast thou laid the foundation of the earth: and the heavens are the work of thy hands" (Ps.102:25).** **"I make a decree, That in every dominion of my kingdom men tremble and fear before the God of Daniel: for he is the living God, and stedfast for ever, and his kingdom that which shall not be destroyed, and his dominion shall be even unto the end" (Da.6:26).** **"But the salvation of the righteous is of the LORD: he is their strength in the time of trouble" (Ps.37:39).**

PROPHET	TIME/PLACE GIVEN	MAIN MESSAGE	PRACTICAL APPLICATION
The UNNAMED PROPHET who rebuked Eli and his house for profaning the temple of the LORD **Known Facts** Delivered a message to Eli the priest (1 S.2:27-34). **Predictions and Messages** 1. The prophecy that each generation of Eli's family would be stricken so that all the men would die in the prime of life (1 S. 2:27-33; esp. v.31). 2. The prophecy that Eli's sons would both die in the same day—a sign that the prophecy concerning Eli's family would come true (1 S.2:34). 3. The prophecy that the LORD would raise up a faithful priest in place of Eli (1 S.2:35-36). **Scripture References** 1 S.2:12-36	**Time** *1085 B.C., when Eli, the priest, was an old man.* **Place** *Shiloh, the central place of worship in Israel prior to the rule of the kings.*	An unnamed prophet was sent by God to pronounce the terrifying judgment against the priestly family of Eli. All three of his sons who were priests, would soon die, and the priesthood of Eli's family was to be transferred to the family of a faithful priest. The unnamed prophet declared three things: 1. He challenged Eli and his sons to remember the history of the priesthood. He pointed out what a privilege it was for priests to approach God and present the offerings to him. For the offerings symbolized the redemption of God's people through the blood of the sacrifice. 2. He pronounced the charge of God against Eli and his sons—that they had scorned the holy things of God and committed immorality. 3. He pronounced the judgment of God against Eli and his sons. The wickedness of Eli and his sons had been so horrible that God was left with no choice. He had to cut them off as priests. **"And there came a man of God unto Eli, and said unto him, Thus saith the LORD,...Wherefore kick ye at my sacrifice and at mine offering, which I have commanded in my habitation; and honourest thy sons above me, to make yourselves fat with the chiefest of all the offerings of Israel my people? Wherefore the LORD God of Israel saith,...Behold, the days come, that I will cut off thine arm, and the arm of thy father's house, that there shall not be an old man in thine house....And this shall be a sign unto thee, that shall come upon thy two sons, on Hophni and Phinehas; in one day they shall die both of them. And I will raise me up a faithful priest, that shall do according to that which is in mine heart and in my mind: and I will build him a sure house; and he shall walk before mine anointed for ever. And it shall come to pass, that every one that is left in thine house shall come and crouch to him for a piece of silver and a morsel of bread, and shall say, Put me, I pray thee, into one of the priests' offices, that I may eat a piece of bread" (1 S.2:27, 29-31, 34-36).**	Judgment upon the immoral and wicked of this world will definitely take place. This is the strong prophetic message of God's Word. Just when the judgment of God is going to fall upon this world is unknown. Just when each of us is going to stand before God, even the minister, is unknown. But the day is definitely coming. The only sure thing that we know about our lives is this: we will die and after that will be the judgment. Judgment is sure, definite, and absolutely certain. Judgment is coming. **"And as it is appointed unto men once to die, but after this the judgment" (He.9:27).** **"When the Son of man shall come in his glory, and all the holy angels with him, then shall he sit upon the throne of his glory: And before him shall be gathered all nations: and he shall separate them one from another, as a shepherd divideth his sheep from the goats: And he shall set the sheep on his right hand, but the goats on the left" (Mt.25:31-33).**

PROPHET	TIME/PLACE GIVEN	MAIN MESSAGE	PRACTICAL APPLICATION
The **UNNAMED PROPHET** who rebuked Israel for fearing the false gods of the Amorites **Known Facts** Delivered a message to the Israelites (Jud.6:8-10). **Predictions and Messages** The message that Israel had been disobedient because they were in fear of the Amorites (Jud.6:8-10). **Scripture References** Jud.6:7-10	**Time** *Approximately 1210 B.C., during the oppression of the Israelites by the Amorites.* **Place** *The southern regions of Israel.*	The LORD raised up a prophet to rebuke the Israelites because the Israelites needed to be warned as never before. For generations, the Israelites had been failing God, turning back time and again to the sins and evil of their neighbors and engaging in their false worship. The prophet rebuked Israel for four specific sins or evils: ➢ The Israelites had forgotten God's salvation, His wonderful deliverance from Egyptian slavery. ➢ The Israelites had forgotten God's deliverance down through the centuries from their oppressors and forgotten His gift of the promised land. ➢ The Israelites had forsaken God, engaging in false worship or idolatry. ➢ The Israelites had refused to listen to God, disobeying Him and breaking His commandments. **"The LORD sent a prophet unto the children of Israel, which said unto them, Thus saith the LORD God of Israel, I brought you up from Egypt, and brought you forth out of the house of bondage; And I delivered you out of the hand of the Egyptians, and out of the hand of all that oppressed you, and drave them out from before you, and gave you their land; And I said unto you, I am the LORD your God; fear not the gods of the Amorites, in whose land ye dwell: but ye have not obeyed my voice" (Jud.6:8-10).**	If we continue in sin—walk day by day disobeying God—a strong rebuke and correction are needed. We need to be awakened, stirred, aroused out of our slumber and hardness of sin. When we sincerely confess our sins and repent, God will deliver us. But we need to learn one truth: we are not to return to our sin. The sin is to be forsaken or left behind, and we are to walk forward, growing more and more in the righteousness of God. If we return to the same sin time and again, continuing in sin, we deserve to be rebuked. **"And Jesus said unto him, No man, having put his hand to the plough, and looking back, is fit for the kingdom of God" (Lu. 9:62).** **"And have no fellowship with the unfruitful works of darkness, but rather reprove them" (Ep. 5:11).** **"Them that sin rebuke before all, that others also may fear" (1 Ti.5:20).**

PROPHET	TIME/PLACE GIVEN	MAIN MESSAGE	PRACTICAL APPLICATION
The UNNAMED PROPHET who rebuked King Ahab of Israel for sparing Ben-Hadad, the evil king of Aram (Syria) **Known Facts** 1. Belonged to the school of the prophets (1 K.20:35). 2. Delivered a message to King Ahab (1 K. 20:39-42). 3. Was known as a prophet (1 K.20:41). **Predictions and Messages** 1. The prophecy that a fellow prophet would be killed by a lion (1 K.20:36). 2. The message that King Ahab had done evil by sparing Ben-Hadad, the evil king of Aram (1 K.20:39-42). **Scripture References** 1 K.20:31-43	**Time** *855 B.C., during the reign of Ahab of Israel and during the ministry of Elijah the prophet.* **Place** *Samaria, the capital of the Northern Kingdom of Israel.*	Under God's instructions, an unnamed prophet sought to disguise himself in order to confront King Ahab. The unnamed prophet ordered a fellow prophet to strike him so that he would appear to be a wounded soldier when he confronted the king. But the fellow prophet refused. As a result, the unnamed prophet predicted the other prophet's death. The next man obeyed and struck the unnamed prophet, wounding him so that his disguise would not be questioned. Disguised as a wounded soldier, the unnamed prophet waited by the road for the king. When Ahab finally arrived and was passing by, the unnamed prophet cried out for a pardon. He told the king that he was in trouble because he had let a prisoner escape. Ahab demonstrated his hard heart by condemning the man. As soon as Ahab had issued his verdict, the prophet stripped off his disguise and pronounced God's condemnation upon Ahab for letting Ben-Hadad, the evil king of Syria, go free. Ahab's life would be demanded in place of the life of Ben-Hadad. **"Then said he unto him, Because thou hast not obeyed the voice of the LORD, behold, as soon as thou art departed from me, a lion shall slay thee. And as soon as he was departed from him, a lion found him, and slew him" (1 K.20:36).** **"And as the king passed by, he cried unto the king: and he said, Thy servant went out into the midst of the battle; and, behold, a man turned aside, and brought a man unto me, and said, Keep this man: if by any means he be missing, then shall thy life be for his life, or else thou shalt pay a talent of silver. And as thy servant was busy here and there, he was gone. And the king of Israel said unto him, So shall thy judgment be; thyself hast decided it" (1 K.20:39-40).**	The lesson we need to learn is that disobedience has consequences. If we disobey God, we stand condemned and will bear the hand of God's judgment. In giving the commandments, God intended good for us. The commandments tell us how to live good, honorable and productive lives that are victorious and conquering. Through obedience, we can live lives that prove to be successful and that bring a sense of fulfillment and satisfaction to the human heart. **"And to you who are troubled rest with us, when the Lord Jesus shall be revealed from heaven with his mighty angels, In flaming fire taking vengeance on them that know not God, and that obey not the gospel of our Lord Jesus Christ: Who shall be punished with everlasting destruction from the presence of the Lord, and from the glory of his power" (2 Th.1:7-9).** **"But if ye will not obey the voice of the LORD, but rebel against the commandment of the LORD, then shall the hand of the LORD be against you, as it was against your fathers" (1 S.12:15).** **"And a curse, if ye will not obey the commandments of the LORD your God, but turn aside out of the way which I command you this day, to go after other gods, which ye have not known" (De.11:28).**

THE PROPHETS

PROPHET	TIME/PLACE GIVEN	MAIN MESSAGE	PRACTICAL APPLICATION
The UNNAMED PROPHET who rebuked King Amaziah of Judah for his idolatry **Known Facts** Delivered a message to King Amaziah of Judah. **Predictions and Messages** 1. The rebuke of King Amaziah for foolishly worshipping the gods of the Edomites (2 Chr.25:15). 2. The prophecy that King Amaziah would be destroyed because he would not listen to the message of the prophet (2 Chr.25:16). **Scripture References** 2 Chr.25:14-16	**Time** *767 B.C., the last year of the reign of King Amaziah of Judah.* **Place** *Jerusalem, the capital of the Southern Kingdom of Judah.*	Almost unbelievably and certainly tragically, Amaziah committed the terrible sin of false worship. As part of the plunder from his victory, the king brought back the idols of Edom, set them up and worshipped them. Why would King Amaziah commit such folly, turning away from the LORD to false idols? Perhaps King Amaziah began to think that he actually had the support of these false gods so he began to worship them in thanksgiving for the victory he had achieved. The anger of the LORD was aroused and burned against Amaziah. God sent a prophet to warn the king by asking him a question: why had the king worshipped false gods, gods that could not save their own people from the hand of Amaziah? Reacting in rage, the king rejected the prophetic warning and threatened the prophet if he continued issuing his message of rebuke. But fearlessly, the prophet issued a final warning: God would judge and destroy the king for his sin and for not heeding the warning. **"Wherefore the anger of the LORD was kindled against Amaziah, and he sent unto him a prophet, which said unto him, Why hast thou sought after the gods of the people, which could not deliver their own people out of thine hand? And it came to pass, as he talked with him, that the king said unto him, Art thou made of the king's counsel? forbear; why shouldest thou be smitten? Then the prophet forbare, and said, I know that God hath determined to destroy thee, because thou hast done this, and hast not hearkened unto my counsel" (2 Chr.25:15-16).**	Believers must guard and keep themselves from idols. What does this mean? An idol is anything that takes first place in a person's life, anything that a person puts before God. An idol is anything that consumes man's focus and concentration, anything that consumes his energy and efforts more than God. A person can make an idol out of anything in this world; a person can take anything and worship it before God; he can allow it to consume his mind and thoughts and life: ⇒ houses ⇒ cars ⇒ lands ⇒ boats ⇒ job ⇒ sports ⇒ position ⇒ money ⇒ spouse ⇒ comfort ⇒ children ⇒ television ⇒ sex ⇒ possessions ⇒ food ⇒ pleasures ⇒ power ⇒ recreation But idols are not gods, no matter what their worshipers may think. There is no other God but One. It is true that people call out to gods, but... • they are gods of their own minds and imaginations, ideas and notions. • they are gods of wood and stone. • they are gods and lords of their own creation. • they have no power to save or deliver. **"Little children, keep yourselves from idols" (1 Jo.5:21).** **"Professing themselves to be wise, they became fools, and changed the glory of the uncorruptible God into an image made like to corruptible man, and to birds, and four-footed beasts, and creeping things" (Ro.1:22-23).**

PROPHET	TIME/PLACE GIVEN	MAIN MESSAGE	PRACTICAL APPLICATION
The UNNAMED PROPHET who rebuked King Jeroboam I for his idolatry **Known Facts** 1. Lived in Judah (1 K. 13:1). 2. Prayed for King Jeroboam and the king's withered hand was healed (1 K.13:6). 3. Commanded by God not to delay—not even to eat or drink—while on his mission (1 K. 13:9). 4. Broke the command of God by visiting and having a meal with an old prophet (1 K.13:19). 5. Was killed by a lion because he disobeyed God's command (1 K.13:24). **Predictions and Messages** 1. The prophecy that a king named Josiah would execute all the false prophets on the altar at Bethel which King Jeroboam had set up for idolatry (1 K.13:2). 2. The prophecy that the altar at Bethel would split apart (1 K.13:3). **Scripture References** 1 K.13:1-25; 2 K.23:15-20	**Time** *931 B.C., the first year of the reign of King Jeroboam I, when the country of Israel had just split into two nations, the Northern Kingdom of Israel and the Southern Kingdom of Judah.* **Place** *Bethel, just north of Jerusalem.*	Just as King Jeroboam was standing by the altar he had set up at Bethel, getting ready to present a false sacrifice, he was suddenly confronted by a young unnamed prophet. The young man prophesied against the altar of false worship established by Jeroboam. The altar and its priests would be destroyed by a future descendant of David named Josiah. To prove that this event would take place, the young prophet gave Jeroboam a sign. The altar would immediately be split apart by the power of God Himself and the ashes would pour out. And so it happened. Pointing to the young man, Jeroboam ordered his guards to arrest him. Instead, another shocking sign happened, which abruptly interrupted the arrest. Jeroboam's hand immediately withered. Terrified, Jeroboam pleaded with the prophet for help. The prophet prayed for the king and his hand was restored. **"And he cried against the altar in the word of the LORD, and said, O altar, altar, thus saith the LORD; Behold, a child shall be born unto the house of David, Josiah by name; and upon thee shall he offer the priests of the high places that burn incense upon thee, and men's bones shall be burnt upon thee. And he gave a sign the same day, saying, This is the sign which the LORD hath spoken; Behold, the altar shall be rent, and the ashes that are upon it shall be poured out" (1 K.13:2-3).**	The lesson for us is strikingly clear: idolatry and false worship do not please the LORD. God totally opposes idolatry and false worship. Idols are not just images made out of wood, stone, metal or some other material. We can make an idol out of anything, for idols are anything that captures our heart more than God. Whatever captivates our hearts, whatever the focus of our hearts is, whatever we give our hearts to, that person or thing becomes our god, our idol. For that person or thing possesses our hearts, our primary interest and attention. As a result, God is denied, ignored or forgotten. **"For the wrath of God is revealed from heaven against all ungodliness and unrighteousness of men, who hold the truth in unrighteousness;...Who changed the truth of God into a lie, and worshipped and served the creature more than the Creator, who is blessed for ever. Amen" (Ro. 1:18, 25).** **"Thou shalt not make unto thee any graven image, or any likeness of any thing that is in heaven above, or that is in the earth beneath, or that is in the water under the earth" (Ex.20:4).** **"Take heed to yourselves, that your heart be not deceived, and ye turn aside, and serve other gods, and worship them" (De.11:16).**

PROPHET	TIME/PLACE GIVEN	MAIN MESSAGE	PRACTICAL APPLICATION
The UNNAMED PROPHET who warned **King Amaziah of Judah not to hire the army of Israel** **Known Facts** Delivered a message to King Amaziah. **Predictions and Messages** 1. The warning that King Amaziah of Judah will meet with disaster if he deploys the troops of Israel into battle (2 Chr. 25:7-8). 2. The message that God has the power to help or to bring defeat (2 Chr.25:8). 3. The message that God is able to supply far more than anything ever lost (2 Chr.25:9). **Scripture References** 2 Chr.25:5-10	**Time** *767 B.C., the last year of the reign of King Amaziah of Judah.* **Place** *Jerusalem, the capital of the Southern Kingdom of Judah.*	King Amaziah of Judah was preparing for war against the age-old enemy of Israel, the Edomites. Amaziah had just hired the armies of Israel to assist him in his battles. But before he could deploy these troops, Amaziah was confronted by a prophet of the LORD who issued a strong warning to the king. The prophet told King Amaziah that he must not allow Israel's mercenary troops to march with him. For the LORD was not with Israel. Living wicked lives and engaging in false worship, the people of the Northern Kingdom had rejected the LORD and were no longer placing their hope in the eternal covenant given to David. They had abandoned the LORD; consequently, the LORD had abandoned them. Still speaking to Amaziah, the prophet continued his warning. If the king marched into battle with the Israelite mercenary soldiers, he would be defeated. Even if he fought courageously against the Edomites, the LORD would make sure he was defeated. For the LORD has the power to help or to overthrow an army. The prophet further assured King Amaziah that God would provide far more plunder—more than enough—to cover his losses if he would just discharge the unbelieving troops. **"But there came a man of God to him, saying, O king, let not the army of Israel go with thee; for the LORD is not with Israel, to wit, with all the children of Ephraim. But if thou wilt go, do it, be strong for the battle: God shall make thee fall before the enemy: for God hath power to help, and to cast down. And Amaziah said to the man of God, But what shall we do for the hundred talents which I have given to the army of Israel? And the man of God answered, The LORD is able to give thee much more than this" (2 Chr.25:7-9).**	Believers are to turn away from evil associations. Close associations always influence us. If we fellowship with godly people, we will be influenced by godliness. But if we fellowship with ungodly people, their ungodliness will influence us. It is impossible to escape the influence of close associations. We all influence each other; and the more closely we are associated, the more we are influenced. If a believer associates with the wicked, eventually the wicked will encourage the believer to join him in his sinful behavior. A godly person is always pulled down, influenced negatively by close associations with those who smoke, take drugs, get drunk, or engage in immoral behavior. No matter who we are or how strong we may be, we will be strongly influenced to participate in the sinful behavior. For this reason the LORD commands us to live lives of *spiritual separation*. Believers are not to fellowship nor become closely associated with the wicked and evil of this earth. We are to be spiritually separated. Living upon the earth, we are to be friends with everyone, unbeliever as well as believer. And we are to be kind, caring, and helpful to everyone. But we are not to form close alliances, associations, or bonds with the wicked and evil of this earth. **"But now I have written unto you not to keep company, if any man that is called a brother be a fornicator, or covetous, or an idolater, or a railer, or a drunkard, or an extortioner; with such an one no not to eat" (1 Co.5:11).** **"Thou shalt not follow a multitude to do evil; neither shalt thou speak in a cause to decline after many to wrest judgment" (Ex.23:2).**

The Prophets

PROPHET	TIME/PLACE GIVEN	MAIN MESSAGE	PRACTICAL APPLICATION
URIJAH (Jehovah/Yahweh is a Light) **Known Facts** 1. Was the son of Shemaiah (Je.26:20). 2. Lived in Kiriath-Jearim (Je.26:20). 3. Prophesied in Judah (Je.26:20-21). 4. Fled to Egypt to escape execution by King Jehoiakim (Je.26:21). 5. Was brought back from Egypt by the king's men and slain (Je.26:22-23). 6. Given the burial of a common criminal (Je.26:23). **Predictions and Messages** Preached messages similar to those of Jeremiah the prophet (Je.26:20). **Scripture References** Je.26:20-23	**Time** *608 B.C., at the beginning of the reign of Jehoiakim, king of Judah.* **Place** *Jerusalem, the capital city of Judah, in the palace of the king.*	All that is known about the messages of Urijah is that they were similar to those of Jeremiah, the prophet. By this one fact, we can know something of what Urijah prophesied. First, Urijah was bound to be a true prophet, proclaiming the messages given him by God. He was not speaking the popular, conscience-soothing messages of the false prophets of that time. Second, Urijah was courageous, warning both king and citizen to repent of their wickedness and false worship or else face the judgment of God. Otherwise, why would the king be so angry and determined to have Urijah executed? Third, we can be sure that Urijah preached the truth of God's Word right up until the day of his martyrdom. **"And there was also a man that prophesied in the name of the LORD, Urijah the son of Shemaiah of Kirjathjearim, who prophesied against this city and against this land according to all the words of Jeremiah" (Je.26:20).**	The preacher must not compromise the Word of God. He must say exactly what God gives him to say. After all, the message is not his, but God's. It is not his to change or alter in the least. Even if it means death, the man of God must not give another message or a watered down version of the truth. He must not seek to say what is popular or more acceptable to his listeners. He must preach the whole counsel of God without regard to circumstances or popular opinion. He must say exactly what God gives him to say. **"And he said unto them, Go ye into all the world, and preach the gospel to every creature" (Mk. 16:15).** **"And daily in the temple, and in every house, they ceased not to teach and preach Jesus Christ" (Ac.5:42).** **"But we preach Christ crucified, unto the Jews a stumblingblock, and unto the Greeks foolishness" (1 Co.1:23).** **"For though I preach the gospel, I have nothing to glory of: for necessity is laid upon me; yea, woe is unto me, if I preach not the gospel! (1 Co.9:16).** **"Preach the word; be instant in season, out of season; reprove, rebuke, exhort with all longsuffering and doctrine" (2 Ti.4:2).**

PROPHET	TIME/PLACE GIVEN	MAIN MESSAGE	PRACTICAL APPLICATION
ZECHARIAH (Jehovah/Yahweh has brought to mind), the son of Jehoiada **Known Facts** 1. Was the son of Jehoiada, the priest (2 Chr.24:20). 2. Was stoned to death because of his message (2 Chr.24:21). **Predictions and Messages** The message that the LORD had forsaken the people of Judah because they had forsaken the LORD and his commandments by their false worship and idolatry (2 Chr. 24:20). **Scripture References** 2 Chr.24:17-22; Mt. 23:34-39; Lu.11:47-51	**Time** *797 B.C., a year before the death of Joash, king of Judah.* **Place** *Jerusalem, the capital city of Judah.*	After the death of Jehoiada, the priest, King Joash, who had led a tremendous revival and spiritual reformation in his younger years, slipped away from the LORD and committed terrible apostasy. Joash listened and gave in to wicked, influential leaders who were false worshipers. Because of their terrible apostasy of turning away to false worship, they stood guilty before the LORD and aroused His anger. God sent prophet after prophet to warn the king, but the king and people stubbornly rejected the prophets of God, refusing to listen to their warnings and refusing to repent. In mercy, however, the LORD made one last attempt to get Joash and the people to repent. The Spirit of the LORD came upon Zechariah with a very special message for the king and the people. They had disobeyed God's commandments and forsaken Him; consequently, the LORD had now forsaken them. But in the depth of their stubborn, stiff-necked rebellion, they still did not repent. Instead, they actually murdered the prophet Zechariah. Furious over the pronouncement of judgment against them, Joash ordered the prophet stoned to death in the very courtyard of the temple itself. Looking up into the eyes of the king as he lay dying, Zechariah pronounced a divine curse upon the king and the people. They were to soon face God's vengeance. The next year, the Arameans (Syrians) attacked and overran the countryside. Joash was killed in battle. **"And the Spirit of God came upon Zechariah the son of Jehoiada the priest, which stood above the people, and said unto them, Thus saith God, Why transgress ye the commandments of the LORD, that ye cannot prosper? because ye have forsaken the LORD, he hath also forsaken you" (2 Chr.24:20).**	How many people have a wonderful beginning in life but a terrible ending? Think of people who have walked through many years of life with upright characters, living honest, moral, and just lives. Yet in the latter years of their lives their character has declined, deteriorated. Some have become immoral and dishonest, even cheating other people. Others are no longer kind and gracious but, rather, unkind, mean-spirited, and reactionary, sometimes even cursing or assaulting those who love and care for them. Whereas they used to live righteous lives and profess to be followers of the LORD, they are now backsliding, living carnal, fleshly lives. They not only ignore the LORD but they also deny Him. They curse His name, use profanity, and tell off-colored jokes. They no longer worship the LORD or are faithful in church attendance. Instead of setting the example that we must listen to the Word of God being taught, they slip into immorality, tearing out the hearts of parents, wives, husbands, children, former pastors, and teachers. Far too many who begin with Christ eventually turn away from Him, committing terrible apostasy against Him. **"And because iniquity shall abound, the love of many shall wax cold" (Mt.24:12).** **"They on the rock *are they*, which, when they hear, receive the word with joy; and these have no root, which for a while believe, and in time of temptation fall away" (Lu.8:13).** **"But now, after that ye have known God, or rather are known of God, how turn ye again to the weak and beggarly elements, whereunto ye desire again to be in bondage" (Ga.4:9).** **"Harden not your hearts, as in the provocation, in the day of temptation in the wilderness: When your fathers tempted me, proved me, and saw my works forty years. Wherefore I was grieved with that generation, and said, They do alway err in their heart; and they have not known my ways. So I sware in my wrath, They shall not enter into my rest.) Take heed, brethren, lest there be in any of you an evil heart of unbelief, in departing from the living God" (He.3:8-12).**

PROPHET	TIME/PLACE GIVEN	MAIN MESSAGE	PRACTICAL APPLICATION
ZECHARIAH (Jehovah/Yahweh has brought to mind), the son of Berechiah **Known Facts** 1. Was the son of Berechiah, the priest (Zec. 1:1). 2. Was the grandson of Iddo, the priest (Ezr. 6:14). 3. Ministered at the same time as Haggai, the prophet (Ezr.5:1; 6:14). 4. Prophesied in Jerusalem after the return from captivity (Zec. 1:1; Ezr.6:16). 5. Helped to restore the temple (Ezr.6:14-15). 6. Saw startling visions of the end times (Zec. 1:7-6:8). **Predictions and Messages** 1. The sermon that the people needed to repent and turn to the LORD (Zec.1:2-6). 2. The vision of the horseman beside the myrtle trees—the promise of restoration of the temple and to Jerusalem (Zec.1:7-17). 3. The vision of the four horns and the four craftsmen—the prophecy of future world powers (Zec.1:18-21). 4. The vision of a man with a measuring line—the prophecy of divine protection for Jerusalem (Zec.2). 5. The vision of Joshua the High Priest being accused and slandered by Satan—a prophecy of the redemption for all Israel (Zec.3). 6. The prophecy of the Messiah, the Savior of the world, the Righteous Branch Who would take away the sins of the land and bring peace (Is.11:1; Zec.3:8-10; Mt.2:23). (cont. on next page)	**Time** *520–518 B.C., during the reign of Darius the Mede, when the Israelites had returned from captivity.* **Place** *Jerusalem, the capital city of the remnant of Israel.*	The people of Israel had just come out of foreign captivity and badly needed to have a strong sense of direction. Zechariah, along with Haggai, the prophet, immediately pointed them to God, greatly encouraging the people to restore the temple so that it might be worthy to be used to worship the LORD. Now it was not just a building project that Zechariah was leading. As a spiritual leader of thousands of exiles who had just returned from captivity, Zechariah realized the great importance of quickly calling the people to genuine worship. He had to ground them firmly in the LORD right away. And so Zechariah encouraged the people time and again to turn to the LORD with their whole heart, to worship the Great Shepherd of their souls. Zechariah helped to lead a very great revival. His many visions and prophecies emphasized the love of a sovereign God for His people, and His desire to uphold them and work in their behalf. For those who were determined to serve God wholeheartedly, they would be supported and sustained by the LORD. He would bring about marvelous things in their future. **"Therefore say thou unto them, Thus saith the LORD of hosts; Turn ye unto me, saith the LORD of hosts, and I will turn unto you, saith the LORD of hosts" (Zec.1:3).** **"Thus saith the LORD of hosts; Let your hands be strong, ye that hear in these days these words by the mouth of the prophets, which were in the day that the foundation of the house of the LORD of hosts was laid, that the temple might be built" (Zec.8:9).**	God is sovereign. He rules over the entire universe. But a person should not think that God is far off in outer space someplace. Coming out of terrible tragedy, it is easy for a person to feel that God is a billion miles away. After a tragedy, it is difficult to have a sense of direction. But it is during hardship that a person needs to seek God like never before and to draw close to Him for understanding, for God cares about our problems. We must always be aware that God is not an unconcerned observer of the world He created. He truly cares about every struggle we go through, and He longs to move in our lives to make the future better, much better than our past. God did not just create the world, wind it up and leave it on its own to fly throughout space with man making out the best he can. God is interested and concerned with the world—so much so that He came to earth in human flesh to show how vitally concerned He is. God would not leave man to grope and grasp in the dark. His call to repentance is not for the purpose of pushing man down but to bring him up, to show man that there is a bright future ahead for those who determine to wholeheartedly serve the LORD. **"Jesus saith unto him, I am the way, the truth, and the life: no man cometh unto the Father, but by me" (Jn.14:6).** **"In my distress I called upon the LORD, and cried to my God: and he did hear my voice out of his temple, and my cry did enter into his ears" (2 S.22:7).** **"When thou art in tribulation, and all these things are come upon thee, even in the latter days, if thou turn to the LORD thy God, and shalt be obedient unto his voice; (For the LORD thy God is a merciful God;) he will not forsake thee, neither destroy thee, nor forget the covenant of thy fathers which he sware unto them" (De.4:30-31).**

PROPHET	TIME/PLACE GIVEN	MAIN MESSAGE	PRACTICAL APPLICATION
ZECHARIAH (cont.) 7. The vision of a golden lampstand and two olive trees—the prophecy of continual anointing for Zerubbabel, who was a type of Christ (Zec.4). 8. The vision of a flying scroll—a declaration that wickedness will be purged from the land (Zec.5:1-4). 9. The vision of a woman in a basket—the prophecy of the rebellion of Babylon in the end times (Zec. 5:5-11). 10. The vision of four chariots—the declaration of God's sovereignty over all nations (Zec.6:1-8). 11. A sermon about the proper attitude for religious ceremony (Zec. 7:4-7). 12. A sermon about loving your neighbor (Zec.7:8-14). 13. The prophecy of God's favor coming upon Jerusalem and Judah (Zec.8:1-17). 14. The prophecy of the salvation of the Gentiles (Zec.8:18-23). 15. The prophecy of God's judgment upon Judah's enemies (Zec. 9:1-10). 16. The prophecy of the Christ's kingly declaration—that the Messiah, the Savior of the world, would enter Jerusalem riding on a young donkey (Zec.9:9; Mt.21:1-11). (Cont. in col.3) **Scripture References** The book of *Zechariah*; Ezr.5:1; 6:14; 8:3, 11, 16		**Predictions and Messages** (cont. from col.1) 17. The prophecy of restoration to all Israel (Zec.9:11–10:12). 18. The illustration of two shepherds' staffs—a prophecy of the rejection of the Messiah, the Great Shepherd (Zec.11). 19. The prophecy that the Messiah, the Savior of the world, would be betrayed for thirty pieces of silver (Zec.11:13). 20. The prophecy that Israel will never again abandon the LORD (Zec.12:1–13:9). 21. The prophecy that the Jews will recognize Jesus Christ as the true Messiah, as their true Savior, in the last days (Zec.12:10-14). 22. The prophecy that in the end times, the LORD will be the only king on the earth (Zec.14).	

PROPHET	TIME/PLACE GIVEN	MAIN MESSAGE	PRACTICAL APPLICATION
ZEPHANIAH (Jehovah/Yahweh is darkness or God hides) **Known Facts** 1. Was the son of Cushi (Zep.1:1). 2. Was a descendant of the righteous King Hezekiah (Zep.1:1). 3. Prophesied to Judah, the Southern Kingdom, helping to lead the way for the religious reforms of Josiah (Zep.1:1). **Predictions and Messages** 1. The prophecy of the coming judgment against Judah and Jerusalem (Zep.1:2-18). 2. The sermon about seeking the LORD to escape His wrath (Zep. 2:1-3). 3. The prophecy of the coming judgment against the Philistines (Zep.2:4-7). 4. The prophecy of the coming judgment against Moab and Ammon (Zep.2:8-11). 5. The prophecy of the coming judgment against Cush (Zep. 2:12). 6. The prophecy of the coming judgment against Assyria (Zep. 2:13-15). 7. The prophecy of the coming judgment against Jerusalem (Zep.3:1-7). 8. The prophecy of the purity of Israel in the last days (Zep.3:8-13; Re.14:1-5). 9. The prophecy of the restoration of Israel and Jerusalem (Zep. 3:14-20). **Scripture References** The book of *Zephaniah*	**Time** *640-609 B.C., during the entire reign of Josiah, king of Judah, who led the last great revival before the fall of Jerusalem in 586 B.C.* **Place** *Judah, the Southern Kingdom of Israel and Jerusalem, the capital city.*	After Manasseh and Amon, two of the most wicked kings in all of Judah's history, God raised up a godly king—Josiah. It was at the tender age of eight that Josiah was crowned king. Obviously, some consistent and righteous believers had a strong, spiritual influence upon young Josiah, for he lived a righteous life in the sight of the LORD. In fact, Scripture says that he followed the godly example of David, never deviating from the righteous example set by the ancient king (2 K.22:2). During his reign, Josiah had one major concern: the restoration of the temple and the true worship of the LORD, the only living and true God (2 K.22:3-7). No doubt, the prophet Zephaniah was one of the people who had a strong spiritual influence on Josiah. Zephaniah called the people to repent and to turn back to God. They had acted no better than their evil neighbors, and the wrath of God was about to be poured out. But there was still a ray of hope if only the people would repent and change their evil ways. Scripture reveals to us that the nation did listen to Zephaniah and the other prophets of that time and that the invasion of Babylon was delayed because of their change of heart (2 Chr.34:27-28). As a result of the messages of Zephaniah and others, Josiah started one of the two great revivals in Israel's history. (The other was by Hezekiah, the ancestor of Zephaniah.) Zephaniah's message announced the coming terrible judgment of God, in very dark words. But there was also promised blessing and a bright future ahead for those who turned to God. **"Gather yourselves together, yea, gather together, O nation not desired; Before the decree bring forth, before the day pass as the chaff, before the fierce anger of the LORD come upon you, before the day of the LORD's anger come upon you. Seek ye the LORD, all ye meek of the earth, which have wrought his judgment; seek righteousness, seek meekness: it may be ye shall be hid in the day of the LORD's anger" (Zep.2:1-3)**	Deep concern for righteousness and for true worship should grip our hearts. For righteousness and true worship determine our destiny, both individually and corporately, as a society and nation. Righteousness builds a character of integrity within people, and righteous individuals build up a nation. If a person is righteous, he is honest, just, true, moral and law-abiding. He keeps the laws of the land and works diligently at his job in order to make a significant contribution to society. Righteousness builds the character of morality and integrity. And when there are enough of us with righteous characters, we build a nation of righteousness, a nation of enormous strength. This can be the experience of any of us. True worship also determines our destiny. If we truly worship the true and living God with a humble and repentant attitude, accepting the sacrifice of His Son, then He will accept us. Think about this glorious truth: The LORD God of the universe, Who sent His Son to die for our sins, is the true and living God who loves us. It is He who is to be worshipped, and He alone. There is a bright future for anyone who turns from sin, lives a righteous life, and truly worships God. **"Awake to righteousness, and sin not; for some have not the knowledge of God: I speak this to your shame" (1 Co.15:34).** **"Teaching us that, denying ungodliness and worldly lusts, we should live soberly, righteously, and godly, in this present world; Looking for that blessed hope, and the glorious appearing of the great God and our Saviour Jesus Christ" (Tit.2:12-13).** **"By the blessing of the upright the city is exalted: but it is overthrown by the mouth of the wicked" (Pr.11:11).**
(cont. on next page)			

PROPHET	TIME/PLACE GIVEN	MAIN MESSAGE	PRACTICAL APPLICATION
ZEPHANIAH (cont.)		"I will gather them that are sorrowful for the solemn assembly, who are of thee, to whom the reproach of it was a burden. Behold, at that time I will undo all that afflict thee: and I will save her that halteth, and gather her that was driven out; and I will get them praise and fame in every land where they have been put to shame. At that time will I bring you again, even in the time that I gather you: for I will make you a name and a praise among all people of the earth, when I turn back your captivity before your eyes, saith the LORD" (Zep.3:18-20).	

TIMELINE OF KINGS, PROPHETS AND HISTORY*

0.25 in

History

DATE BC	FOREIGN KINGS	WORLD EVENTS
1000	Ashur-Rabi II (1010–970) (Assyria) Hiram (1003–966) (Tyre) Tiglath-Pileser II (960–935) (Assyria)	David captures Jerusalem (1004) Foundation for the Temple (966) 22nd Egyptian Dynasty (945) Kingdom Divided (930)
950		
930		
	Shishak I (945–924) (Egypt)	Assyria makes peace with Babylon (915)
900	Ben-Hadad I (900) (Syria) Eth-Baal (887–856) (Sidon)	Jehoshaphat leads a revival (865) Elijah's contest with prophets of Baal (857) Elijah's mantle passed to Elisha (845)
850	Hazael (840) (Syria)	Carthage established (814) Joash repairs Temple (812) 23rd Egyptian dynasty (800)
800	Ben-Hadad II (798) (Syria) Ben-Hadad III (773) (Syria)	Olympic games begin (776) Rome founded (753)
750	Rezin (750) (Syria)	Babylonian and Chinese calendar (750)

The United Kingdom

BIBLE REF.	KINGS (YEARS REIGNED)	PROPHETS
1 S.16:1–1 K.2:11; 1 Chr.11:1-30	David (40) (1011–971)	Samuel (1095–1015) Gad (1015–950) Asaph (1004)
1 K.2:12–11:43; 1 Chr.28:1–2 Chr.9:31	Solomon (40) (971–931)	Natthan (1003–931) Heman (971)

The Divided Kingdom

Southern Kingdom of Judah

BIBLE REF.	KINGS (YEARS REIGNED)	PROPHETS
1 K.12:1-24; 14:21-31; 2 Chr.9:31-12:16	Rehoboam (17) (931–913)	
1 K.15:1-8; 2 Chr.12:16-14:1	Abijah (3) (913–911)	
1 K.15:9-24; 2 Chr.14:1-16:14	Asa (3) (911–870)	Iddo (910) Azariah (896)
1 K.22:41-50; 2 K.3:6-14; 2 Chr.17:1-21:1	Jehoshaphat (25) (873–848)	
2 K.8:16-24; 2 Chr.21:1-20	Jehoram (8) (853–841)	
2 K.8:25-29; 9:27-29; 2 Chr.22:1-10	Ahaziah (2) (841)	Obadiah (845)
2 K.11:1-16; 2 Chr.22:10-23:21	Athaliah (7) (841–835)	
2 K.11:17-12:21; 2 Chr.22:11-12; 24:1-27	Joash/Jehoash (40) (835–796)	Joel (830)
2 K.14:1-20; 2 Chr.24:27-25:28	Amaziah (29) (796–767)	
2 K.14:21-22; 15:1-7; 2 Chr.26:1-23	Azariah/Uzziah (52) (792–740)	Hosea (788–723) Jonah (780–765)
2 K.15:32-38; 2 Chr.26:23-27:9	Jotham (16) (750–731)	

Northern Kingdom of Israel

PROPHETS	KINGS (YEARS REIGNED)	BIBLE REF.
Ahijah (931–910) Man from Judah (930) Shemaiah (927)	Jeroboam I (22) (931–910)	1 K.12:1-24; 12:25-14:20; 2 Chr.10:1-16
Jehu (886)	Nadab (2) (910–909)	1 K.15:25-31
	Baasha (24) (909–886)	1 K.15:16-16:7; 2 Chr.16:1-6
	Elah (2) (886–885)	1 K.16:6-14
Hanani (870)	Zimri (7 days) (885)	1 K.16:9-20
	Omri (12) (885–874)	1 K.16:21-28
Elijah (860–845)	Ahab (22) (874–853)	1 K.16:28-22:40; 2 Chr.18:1-34
Micaiah (853) Elisha (850–795) Eliezer (849–48)	Ahaziah (2) (853–852)	1 K.22:49-51; 2 K.1:1-18; 2 Chr.20:35-37; 22:1-11
	Joram/Jehoram (12) (852–841)	2 K.1:17; 3:1-8:15
	Jehu (28) (841–814)	2 K.9:1,10:36; 2 Chr.22:7-9
	Jehoahaz (17) (814–798)	2 K.13:1-9
Zechariah (797)	Jehoash (16) (798–782)	2 K.13:9-25; 14:8-16
Jonah (780–765)	Jeroboam II (41) (793–753)	2 K.14:23-29
Amos (750)	Zechariah (6 mos) (753)	2 K.15:8-12
	Shallum (1 mo) (752)	2 K.15:13-15
	Menahem (10) (752–742)	2 K.15:16-22

THE DIVIDED KINGDOM

SOUTHERN KINGDOM OF JUDAH			NORTHERN KINGDOM OF ISRAEL			DATE BC	HISTORY	
BIBLE REF.	KINGS (YEARS REIGNED)	PROPHETS	BIBLE REF.	KINGS (YEARS REIGNED)	PROPHETS		FOREIGN KINGS	WORLD EVENTS
2 K.15:38-16:20; 2 Chr.27:9-27; Is.7:1-9:1	Ahaz (16) (735–715)	Isaiah (740–690)	2 K.15:23-26	Pekahiah (2) (742–740)			Tiglath-Pil[n]eser III [or Pul] (745–721) (Assyria)	Assyria takes control of Northern Kingdom (745–627)
		Micah (735–725)	2 K.15:27-31	Pekah (20) (752–732) (ruled only in Gilead) (740–732) (ruled in Samaria)			Shallmaneser V (727–722) (Assyria)	Assyria invades Northern Israel (732)
		Oded (733)					So (727–716) (Egypt)	
2 K.18:1-20:21; 2 Chr.28:27-32:33; Ps.25:1. Is.36:1-39:8	Hezekiah (29) (729–686)		2 K.17:1-23	Hoshea (9) (732–722)			Sargon II (710–705) (Assyria)	Fall of Northern Kingdom (722)
							Sennacherib (705–681) (Assyria)	Sennacherib defeats Egypt (701) / Hezekiah's tunnel (701)
							Merodach-Baladan (721–710, 705–704) (Assyria)	
						700	Tirhakah (690–664) (Egypt)	185,000 Assyrians killed by God (701)
2 K.20:21-21:18; 2 Chr.32:33-33:20	Manasseh (55) (696–642)							Sennacherib destroys Babylon
2 K.21:18-26; 2 Chr.33:20-25	Amon (2) (642–640)	Nahum (663–612)					Esarhaddon (681–669) (Assyria)	Josiah's reform (621)
						650	Nabopolassar (626–605) (Assyria)	Nineveh destroyed (612)
2 K.21:26-23:30; 2 Chr.33:25-35:27	Josiah (31) (640–609)	Zephaniah (640–609)					Neco (610–595) (Egypt)	Battle of Carchemish (605)
2 K.23:31-33; 2 Chr.36:1-4	Jehoaz/Jehoahaz (3 mos) (609)	Jeremiah (627–562)						1st group of exiles from Judah taken to Babylon (605)
2 K.23:34-24:7; 2 Chr.36:5-8	Jehoiakim (11) (608–598)	Habakkuk (615–598)					Nebuchadnezzar II (605–562) (Babylon)	
2 K.24:8-17; 25:27-30; 2 Chr.36:8-10;	Jehoiachin (3 mos) (598–597)	Daniel (605–535)				600		2nd group of exiles from Judah taken to Babylon (597)
2 K.24:18-25:21; 2 Chr.36:10-14; Je.21:1-52:11	Zedekiah/Mattaniah (11) (597–586)	Ezekiel (593–571)						Fall of Judah—Third group of exiles from Judah taken to Babylon (586)
2 K.25:22-26; Je.40:5-41:18	Gedaliah (2 mos) (Appointed by Nebuchadnezzar) (586)						Evil-Merodach (562–560) (Babylon)	
						550	Cyrus II (559–530) (Medo-Persia)	Fall of Babylon to Medo-Persian Empire (539)
							Belshazzar (552–539) (Babylon)	Cyrus II decrees that the Jews may return to the Holy Land (538)
		Haggai (520)						1st exiles return to Holy Land with Zerubbabel (537)
		Zechariah (520–518)						1st Temple foundation laid (536) / 2nd Temple foundation laid (520)
						500	Darius I (521–486) (Medo-Persia)	Temple completed (516) / Republic of Rome est. (509)
		Malachi (430)				450	Artaxerxes (465–425) (Persia)	2nd return under Ezra (458)
								3rd return under Nehemiah (445)

*Some dates are approximate.

The resources used for the Timeline are as follows:

1 The Bible
2 Archer, Gleason L. Encyclopedia of Bible Difficulties. (Grand Rapids, Michigan: Zondervan Publishing House), 1982.
3 Freedman, David Noel, ed., et. al. The Anchor Bible Dictionary. (New York: Doubleday), 1992.
4 Grun, Bernard. The Timetables of History. 3rd ed. (New York: Simon & Schuster), 1991.
5 Kaiser, Walter C. A History of Israel. (Nashville, Tennessee: Broadman & Holman Publishers), 1998.
6 Silverman, David P., ed. Ancient Egypt. (New York: Oxford University Press), 1997.

ACKNOWLEDGMENTS AND BIBLIOGRAPHY

Every child of God is precious to the LORD and deeply loved. And every child as a servant of the LORD touches the lives of those who come in contact with him or his ministry. The writing ministries of the following servants have touched this work, and we are grateful that God brought their writings our way. We hereby acknowledge their ministry to us, being fully aware that there are so many others down through the years whose writings have touched our lives and who deserve mention, but whose names have faded from our memory. May our wonderful LORD continue to bless the ministries of these dear servants—and the ministries of us all—as we diligently labor to reach the world for Christ and to meet the desperate needs of those who suffer so much.

THE REFERENCE WORKS

Aharoni, Yohanan, Michael Avi-Yonah, Anson F. Rainey and Ze'ev Safrai, Editors. *The MacMillan Bible Atlas*, 3rd Ed. Jerusalem: Carta, The Israel Map and Publishing Company, 1993.

Albright, W.F. *History, Archaeology and Christian Humanism.* New York: McGraw Hill, 1964.

Archer, Gleason L. *A Survey of Old Testament Introduction.* Chicago, IL: Moody Bible Institute of Chicago, 1974.

_____. *Encyclopedia of Bible Difficulties.* Grand Rapids, Michigan: Zondervan Publishing House, 1982.

Atlas of the World. Hammond Concise Edition. Maplewood, NJ: Hammond Inc., 1993.

Baker's Dictionary of Theology. Everett F. Harrison, Editor-in-Chief. Grand Rapids, MI: Baker Book House, 1960.

Barker, William P. *Everyone in the Bible.* Westwood, NJ: Fleming H. Revell Co., 1966.

Benware, Paul N. *Survey of the Old Testament.* "Everyman's Bible Commentary." Chicago, IL: Moody Bible Institute of Chicago, 1993.

Bromiley, Geoffrey W., Editor, et. al. *David.* "The International Standard Bible Encyclopedia." Grand Rapids, MI: Eerdmans Publishing Co., 1988.

Brown, Francis. *The New Brown-Driver-Briggs-Gesenius Hebrew-English Lexicon.* Peabody, MA: Hendrickson Publishers, 1979.

Cruden's Complete Concordance of the Old & New Testament. Philadelphia, PA: The John C. Winston Co., 1930.

Dake, Finis Jennings. *Dake's Annotated Reference Bible, The Holy Bible.* Lawrenceville, GA: Dake Bible Sales, Inc., 1963.

Douglas, J.D. Editor. *New Bible Dictionary.* Wheaton, IL: Tyndale House Publishers, Inc., 1982.

Easton's 1897 Bible Dictionary. Database NavPress Software, 1996.

Elwell, Walter A., Editor. *The Evangelical Dictionary of Theology.* Grand Rapids, MI: Baker Book House, 1984.

Enhanced Nave's Topics. Database NavPress Software, 1991, 1994.

Frank, Harry Thomas, ed. *Atlas of the Bible Lands.* Maplewood, NJ: Hammond Incorporated, 1977.

Freedman, David Noel, Editor, et. al. *The Anchor Bible Dictionary.* New York: Doubleday, 1992.

Funk & Wagnalls Standard Desk Dictionary. Lippincott & Crowell, Publishers, 1980, Vol.2.

Geisler, Norman. *A Popular Survey of the Old Testament.* Grand Rapids, MI: Baker Book House, 1977.

Gill, Dr. A.L., Compiler. *God's Promises For Your Every Need.* Dallas, TX: Word Publishing, 1995.

Good News Bible. Old Testament: © American Bible Society, 1976. New Testament: © American Bible Society, 1966, 1971, 1976. Collins World.

Good News for Modern Man, The New Testament. New York, NY: American Bible Society, 1971.

Goodrick, Edward W. and John R. Kohlenberger, III. *The NIV Exhaustive Concordance.* Grand Rapids, MI: Zondervan Publishing House, 1990.

Grun, Bernard. *The Timetables of History.* 3rd Edition. New York: Simon & Schuster, 1991.

Harrison, Roland Kenneth. *Introduction to the Old Testament.* Grand Rapids, MI: Eerdmans Publishing Co., 1969.

Holman Bible Dictionary. Nashville, TN: Broadman & Holman Publishers, 1991. Database NavPress Software.

Hooper, Jerry L., Editor. *The Holman Bible Atlas.* Philadelphia, PA: A.J. Holman Company, 1978.

ISBE. Grand Rapids, MI: Eerdmans Publishing Co., 1988.

Josephus, Flavius. *Complete Works.* Grand Rapids, MI: Kregel Publications, 1981.

Kaiser, Walter C. *A History of Israel.* Nashville, Tennessee: Broadman and Holman Publishers, 1998.

Kipfer, Barbara Ann, Ph.D. *Roget's 21st Century Thesaurus.* New York, NY: Dell Publishing, 1992.

Kohlenberger, John R. III. *The Interlinear NIV Hebrew-English Old Testament.* Grand Rapids, MI: Zondervan Publishing House, 1987.

Kouffman, Donald T. *The Dictionary of Religious Terms.* Westwood, NJ: Fleming H. Revell Co., 1967.

Life Application® Bible. Wheaton, IL: Tyndale House Publishers, Inc., 1991.

Life Application® Study Bible. New International Version. Tyndale House Publishers, Inc.: Wheaton, IL 1991, and Zondervan Publishing House: Grand Rapids, MI, 1984.

Lindsell, Harold and Woodbridge, Charles J. *A Handbook of Christian Truth.* Westwood, NJ: Fleming H. Revell Company, A Division of Baker Book House, 1953.

Living Quotations For Christians. Edited by Sherwood Eliot Wirt and Kersten Beckstrom. New York, NY: Harper & Row, Publishers, 1974.

Lockyer, Herbert. *All the Books and Chapters of the Bible.* Grand Rapids, MI: Zondervan Publishing House, 1966.

_____. *All the Kings and Queens of the Bible.* Grand Rapids, MI: Zondervan Publishing House, 1961.

_____. *All the Men of the Bible.* Grand Rapids, MI: Zondervan Publishing House, 1958.

_____. *All the Miracles of the Bible.* Grand Rapids, MI: Zondervan Publishing House, 1961.

_____. *All the Parables of the Bible.* Grand Rapids, MI: Zondervan Publishing House, 1963.

_____. *The Women of the Bible.* Grand Rapids, MI: Zondervan Publishing House, 1967.

Luckenbill, Daniel David. *Ancient Records of Assyria and Babylonia*, 2 Vols. (ARAB) London: Histories and Mysteries of Man Ltd., 1989.

Martin, Alfred. *Survey of the Scriptures*, Part I, II, III. Chicago, IL: Moody Bible Institute of Chicago, 1961.

McDowell, Josh. *Evidence That Demands a Verdict*, Vol.1. San Bernardino, CA: Here's Life Publishers, Inc., 1979.

Miller, Madeleine S. & J. Lane. *Harper's Bible Dictionary*. New York, NY: Harper & Row Publishers, 1961.

Nave, Orville J. *Nave's Topical Bible*. Nashville, TN: The Southwestern Company. Copyright © by J.B. Henderson, 1921.

Nelson's Complete Book of Bible Maps & Charts. Nashville, TN: Thomas Nelson Publishers, Inc., 1996.

New American Standard Bible, Updated Edition. La Habra, CA: The Lockman Foundation, 1995.

New Bible Dictionary, 3rd Edition. Leicester, England: Universities & Colleges Christian Fellowship, 1996.

New Living Translation, Holy Bible. Wheaton, IL: Tyndale House Publishers, Inc., 1996.

NIV Thompson Student Bible. Jauchen, John S., Editor, et. al. Indianapolis, IN: Kirkbride Bible Company, 1999.

Orr, James, Editor. *The International Standard Bible Encyclopaedia*, Grand Rapids, MI: Eerdmans Publishing Co., 1939.

Orr, William. *How We May Know That God Is*. Wheaton, IL: Van Kampen Press, n.d.

Owens, John Joseph. *Analytical Key to the Old Testament,* Vols.1, 2, 3. Grand Rapids, MI: Baker Book House, 1989.

Payne, J. Barton. *Encyclopedia of Biblical Prophecy*. New York, NY: Harper & Row, Publishers, 1973.

Pilgrim Edition, Holy Bible. New York, NY: Oxford University Press, 1952.

Ridout, Samuel. *Lectures on the Tabernacle*. New York, NY: Loizeaux Brothers, Inc., 1914.

Silverman, David P. ed. *Ancient Egypt*. New York: Oxford University Press, 1997.

Smith, William. *Smith's Bible Dictionary*. Peabody, MA: Hendrickson Publishers, n.d.

Stone, Nathan J. *Names of God*. Chicago, IL: Moody Press, 1944.

Strong, James. *Strong's Exhaustive Concordance of the Bible*. Nashville, TN: Thomas Nelson, Inc., 1990.

———. *The Tabernacle of Israel*. Grand Rapids, MI: Kregel Publications, 1987.

Strong's Greek and Hebrew Dictionary as compiled by iExalt Software. Database NavPress Software, 1990-1993.

The Amplified Bible. Scripture taken from THE AMPLIFIED BIBLE, Old Testament copyright © 1965, 1987 by the Zondervan Publishing House. The Amplified New Testament copyright © 1958, 1987 by The Lockman Foundation. Used by permission.

The Holy Bible in Four Translations. Minneapolis, MN: Worldwide Publications. Copyright © The Iversen-Norman Associates: New York, NY, 1972.

The Illustrated Bible Atlas, with Historical Notes by F. F. Bruce. Grand Rapids, MI: Kregel Publications, 1994.

The Interlinear Bible, Vols.1, 2, 3. Translated by Jay P. Green, Sr. Grand Rapids, MI: Baker Book House, 1976.

The Interpreter's Bible, 12 Vols. New York, NY: Abingdon Press, 1956.

The NASB Greek/Hebrew Dictionary and Concordance. La Habra, CA: The Lockman Foundation, 1988.

The Nelson Study Bible, New King James Version. Earl D. Radmacher, General Editor. Nashville, TN: Thomas Nelson Publishers, Inc., 1997.

The New Compact Bible Dictionary. Edited by T. Alton Bryant. Grand Rapids, MI: Zondervan Publishing House, 1967. Used by permission of Zondervan Publishing House.

The New Scofield Reference Bible. Edited by C.I. Scofield. New York, NY: Oxford University Press, 1967.

The New Testament-English, PI-RHO. "The Complete Biblical Library." Springfield, MO: World Library Press Inc, 1991.

The New Thompson Chain Reference Bible. Indianapolis, IN: B.B. Kirkbride Bible Co., Inc., 1964.

The New Unger's Bible Dictionary. Chicago, IL: Moody Press, 1998. Database NavPress Software, 1997.

The NIV Study Bible, New International Version. Grand Rapids, MI: Zondervan Publishing House, 1985.

The Old Testament Hebrew-English Dictionary, NUN—AYIN. "The Complete Biblical Library." Springfield, MO: World Library Press Inc., 1999.

The Open Bible. Nashville, TN: Thomas Nelson Publishers, 1977.

The Quest Study Bible. New International Version. Grand Rapids, MI: Zondervan Publishing House, 1994.

The Zondervan Pictorial Encyclopedia of the Bible, Vol.1. Merrill C. Tenney, Editor. Grand Rapids, MI: Zondervan Publishing House, 1982.

Theological Wordbook of the Old Testament. Edited by R. Laird Harris. Chicago, IL: Moody Bible Institute of Chicago, 1980.

Unger, Merrill F. & William White, Jr. *Nelson's Expository Dictionary of the Old Testament*. Nashville, TN: Thomas Nelson Publishers, 1980.

Vine, W.E., Merrill F. Unger, William White, Jr. *Vine's Complete Expository Dictionary of Old and New Testament Words*. Nashville, TN: Thomas Nelson Publishers, 1985.

Walton, John H. *Chronological and Background Charts of the Old Testament*. Grand Rapids, MI: Zondervan Publishing House, 1978.

Webster's Seventh New Collegiate Dictionary. Springfield, MA: G. & C. Merriam Company, Publishers, 1971.

Wilmington. Harold L. *The Outline Bible*. Wheaton, IL: Tyndale House Publishers, Inc., 1999.

Wilson, William. *Wilson's Old Testament Word Studies*. McLean, VA: MacDonald Publishing Company, n.d.

Wood, Leon. *A Survey of Israel's History*. Grand Rapids, MI: Zondervan Publishing House, 1982.

Young, Edward J. *An Introduction to the Old Testament*. Grand Rapids, MI: Eerdmans Publishing Co., 1964.

Young, Robert. *Young's Analytical Concordance to the Bible*. Grand Rapids, MI: Eerdmans Publishing Co., n.d.

Zodhiates, Spiros, Th.D., Executive Editor. *The Hebrew-Greek Key Study Bible, New International Version*. Chattanooga, TN: AMG Publishers, 1996.

Zondervan NIV Bible Library. Version 2.5. Grand Rapids, MI: Zondervan Publishing House.

THE COMMENTARIES

Alexander, Joseph Addison. *The Prophecies of Isaiah.* "The Zondervan Commentary Series." Grand Rapids, MI: Zondervan Publishing House, 1981.

Bultema, Harry. *Isaiah.* Grand Rapids, MI: Kregel Publications, 1981.

Burroughs, P.E., D.D. *Old Testament Studies.* Nashville, TN: Sunday School Board, Southern Baptist Convention, 1915.

Clements, R.E. *Isaiah 1-39.* "The New Century Bible Commentary." Grand Rapids, MI: Eerdmans Publishing Co., 1980.

Criswell, W.A. *Isaiah an exposition.* Grand Rapids, MI: Zondervan Publishing House, 1977.

Elwell, Walter A., Editor. *Topical Analysis of the Bible.* (Grand Rapids, MI: Baker Book House, 1991.

Evans, Mary J. *1 and 2 Samuel.* "New International Biblical Commentary." Peabody, MA: Hendrickson Publishers, Inc., 2000.

Griffin, Gilbert L. *The Gospel in Isaiah.* Nashville, TN: Convention Press, 1968.

Grogan, G.W. *Isaiah.* "The Expositor's Bible Commentary," Vol.6. Grand Rapids, MI: Zondervan Publishing House, 1988.

Henry, Matthew. *Matthew Henry's Commentary*, 6 Vols. Old Tappan, NJ: Fleming H. Revell Co., n.d.

Holladay, William L. *Isaiah: Scroll of a Prophetic Heritage.* Grand Rapids, MI: Eerdmans Publishing Co., 1978.

Horton, Stanley M. *Isaiah.* "The Complete Biblical Library: The Old Testament," Vol.9. Springfield, MO: World Library Press Inc., 1995.

Ironside, H.A. *The Prophet Isaiah.* Neptune, NJ: Loizeaux Brothers, Inc., 1952.

Jennings, F.C. *Studies in Isaiah.* Neptune, NJ: Loizeaux Brothers, Inc., n.d..

Kaiser, Walter C., Jr. *A History of Israel.* Nashville, TN: Broadman & Holman Publishers, 1998.

Keil-Delitzsch. *Commentary on the Old Testament*, Vol.8. Grand Rapids, MI: Eerdmans Publishing Co., n.d.

Kirkpatrick, A.F., General Editor. *The Book of the Prophet Isaiah Chapters I-XXXIX.* "The Cambridge Bible for Schools and Colleges." New York, NY: Cambridge University Press, 1958.

———. *The Book of the Prophet Isaiah Chapters XL-LXVI.* "The Cambridge Bible for Schools and Colleges." New York, NY: Cambridge University Press, 1960.

Leupold, H.C. *Exposition of Isaiah,* Vol.1. Baker Book House, Grand Rapids, Michigan, 1968.

Maclaren, Alexander. *Expositions of Holy Scripture*, 11 Vols. Grand Rapids, MI: Eerdmans Publishing Co., 1952-59.

Martin, Alfred. *Isaiah, The Salvation of Jehovah.* "Everyman's Bible Commentary." Chicago, IL: Moody Bible Institute of Chicago, 1956.

McGee, J. Vernon. *Thru the Bible*, Vol.3. Nashville, TN: Thomas Nelson Publishers, 1982.

McKenna, David. *Isaiah 1-39.* "Mastering the Old Testament," Vol.16A. Dallas, TX: Word Publishing, 1994.

Morgan, G. Campbell. *Living Messages of the Books of the Bible*, Vol.1. Old Tappan, NJ: Fleming H. Revell, 1912.

Morris, Henry M. *The Genesis Record.* Grand Rapids, MI., 1996.

Motyer, J. Alec. *Isaiah .*"The Tyndale Old Testament Commentaries." Downers Grove, IL: Inter-Varsity Press, 1999.

———. *The Prophecy of Isaiah.* Downers Grove, IL: Inter-varsity Press, 1993.

Oswalt, John N. *Isaiah 1-39.* "The New International Commentary on the Old Testament," Grand Rapids, MI: Eerdmans Publishing Co. 1982.

Poole, Matthew. *Matthew Poole's Commentary on the Holy Bible*, Vol.2. Peabody, MA: Hendrickson Publishers, n.d.

Redpath, Alan. *Victorious Christian Service.* Westwood, NJ: Fleming H. Revell Co., 1958.

Schulz, Samuel J. *The Old Testament Speaks*, 4th Edition. San Francisco, CA: Harper Collins Publishers, 1990.

Smith, James E. *What the Bible Teaches about the Promised Messiah.* Nashville, TN: Thomas Nelson Publishers, 1993.

Spurgeon, C.H. *Spurgeon's Sermon Notes. Genesis to Malachi.* Westwood, NJ: Fleming H. Revell Co., n.d.

The Pulpit Commentary. 23 Vols. Edited by H.D.M. Spence & Joseph S. Exell. Grand Rapids, MI: Eerdmans Publishing Co., 1950.

Walvoord, John F. and Roy B. Zuck, Editors. *The Bible Knowledge Commentary, Old Testament.* Colorado Springs, CO: Chariot Victor Publishing, 1985.

Wiersbe, Warren W. *Be Comforted.* Wheaton, IL: Victor Books, 1992.

Willis, John T. *Isaiah.* "The Living Word Commentary on the Old Testament." Abilene, TX: ACU Press, 1984.

Wright, G. Ernest. *Isaiah.* "The Layman's Bible Commentary," Vol.11. Atlanta, GA: John Knox Press, 1964.

Young, Edward J. *The Book of Isaiah,* Vol.1. Grand Rapids, MI: Eerdmans Publishing Co., 1965.

OUTLINE BIBLE RESOURCES

This material, like similar works, has come from imperfect man and is thus susceptible to human error. We are nevertheless grateful to God for both calling us and empowering us through His Holy Spirit to undertake this task. Because of His goodness and grace, *The Preacher's Outline & Sermon Bible*® New Testament and Old Testament volumes are now complete.

The Minister's Personal Handbook, The Believer's Personal Handbook, and other helpful **Outline Bible Resources** are available in printed form as well as releasing electronically on various software programs.

God has given the strength and stamina to bring us this far. Our confidence is that as we keep our eyes on Him and remain grounded in the undeniable truths of the Word, we will continue to produce other helpful Outline Bible Resources for God's dear servants to use in their Bible Study and discipleship.

We offer this material, first, to Him in whose Name we labor and serve and for whose glory it has been produced, and, second, to everyone everywhere who preaches and teaches the Word.

Our daily prayer is that each volume will lead thousands, millions, yes, even billions, into a better understanding of the Holy Scriptures and a fuller knowledge of Jesus Christ the Incarnate Word, of whom the Scriptures so faithfully testify.

You will be pleased to know that Leadership Ministries Worldwide partners with Christian organizations, printers, and mission groups around the world to make Outline Bible Resources available and affordable in many countries and foreign languages. It is our goal that *every* leader around the world, both clergy and lay, will be able to understand God's Holy Word and to present God's message with more clarity, authority, and understanding—all beyond his or her own power.

LEADERSHIP MINISTRIES WORLDWIDE
PO Box 21310 • Chattanooga, TN 37424-0310
(423) 855-2181 • FAX (423) 855-8616
info@lmw.org
www.lmw.org - FREE Download materials

LEADERSHIP MINISTRIES WORLDWIDE

Publishers of Outline Bible Resources

• THE PREACHER'S OUTLINE & SERMON BIBLE® (POSB) • KJV – NIV

NEW TESTAMENT

Matthew 1 (chapters 1–15)
Matthew 2 (chapters 16–28)
Mark
Luke
John
Acts
Romans

1 & 2 Corinthians
Galatians, Ephesians, Philippians, Colossians
1 & 2 Thessalonians, 1 & 2 Timothy, Titus, Philemon
Hebrews, James
1 & 2 Peter, 1, 2, & 3 John, Jude
Revelation
Master Outline & Subject Index

OLD TESTAMENT

Genesis 1 (chapters 1–11)
Genesis 2 (chapters 12–50)
Exodus 1 (chapters 1–18)
Exodus 2 (chapters 19–40)
Leviticus
Numbers
Deuteronomy
Joshua
Judges, Ruth
1 Samuel
2 Samuel

1 Kings
2 Kings
1 Chronicles
2 Chronicles
Ezra, Nehemiah, Esther, Job
Psalms 1 (chapters 1-41)
Psalms 2 (chapters 42-106)
Psalms 3 (chapters 107-150)
Proverbs
Ecclesiastes, Song of Solomon

Isaiah 1 (chapters 1-35)
Isaiah 2 (chapters 36-66)
Jeremiah 1 (chapters 1-29)
Jeremiah 2 (chapters 30-52),
   Lamentations
Ezekiel
Daniel, Hosea
Joel, Amos, Obadiah, Jonah,
   Micah, Nahum
Habakkuk, Zephaniah, Haggai,
   Zechariah, Malachi

Print versions of all Outline Bible Resources are available in various forms.

- *What the Bible Says to the Believer* — **The Believer's Personal Handbook**
  11 Chs. – Over 500 Subjects, 300 Promises, & 400 Verses Expounded - Italian Imitation Leather or Paperback
- *What the Bible Says to the Minister* — **The Minister's Personal Handbook**
  12 Chs. - 127 Subjects - 400 Verses Expounded - Italian Imitation Leather or Paperback
- **Practical Word Studies In the New Testament** — 2 Vol. Hardcover Set
- **The Teacher's Outline & Study Bible™ - Various New Testament Books**
  Complete 30 - 45 minute lessons – with illustrations and discussion questions
- **Practical Illustrations — Companion to the POSB**
  Arranged by topic and Scripture reference
- **What the Bible Says About Series – Various Subjects**
- **OBR on various digital platforms**
  See current digital providers on our website at www.lmw.org
- **Translations of various books**
  See our website for more information or contact our office

— Contact LMW for quantity orders and information —

LEADERSHIP MINISTRIES WORLDWIDE or Your Local Christian Bookstore
PO Box 21310 • Chattanooga, TN 37424-0310
(423) 855-2181 • FAX (423) 855-8616 (Mon. - Thurs. 9am – 5pm Eastern)
E-mail - info@lmw.org • Order online at www.lmw.org

PURPOSE STATEMENT

LEADERSHIP MINISTRIES WORLDWIDE

exists to equip ministers, teachers, and laymen in their understanding, preaching, and teaching of God's Word by publishing and distributing worldwide *The Preacher's Outline & Sermon Bible*® and related **Outline Bible Resources**; to reach & disciple men, women, boys and girls for Jesus Christ.

MISSION STATEMENT

1. To make the Bible so understandable – its truth so clear and plain – that men and women everywhere, whether teacher or student, preacher or hearer, can grasp its message and receive Jesus Christ as Savior, and…

2. To place the Bible in the hands of all who will preach and teach God's Holy Word, verse by verse, precept by precept, regardless of the individual's ability to purchase it.

The **Outline Bible Resources** have been given to LMW for printing and especially distribution worldwide at/below cost, by those who remain anonymous. One fact, however, is as true today as it was in the time of Christ:

THE GOSPEL IS FREE, BUT THE COST OF TAKING IT IS NOT

LMW depends on the generous gifts of believers with a heart for Him and a love for the lost. They help pay for the printing, translating, and distributing of **Outline Bible Resources** into the hands of God's servants worldwide, who will present the Gospel message with clarity, authority, and understanding beyond their own.

LMW was incorporated in the state of Tennessee in July 1992 and received IRS 501 (c)(3) nonprofit status in March 1994. LMW is an international, nondenominational mission organization. All proceeds from USA sales, along with donations from donor partners, go directly to underwrite our translation and distribution projects of **Outline Bible Resources** to preachers, church and lay leaders, and Bible students around the world.

www.ingramcontent.com/pod-product-compliance
Lightning Source LLC
Chambersburg PA
CBHW081259040426

42452CB00014B/2564